Peace
of
Mind

www.transworldbooks.co.uk

Peace of Mind

Becoming Fully Present

Thich Nhat Hanh

BANTAM PRESS

LONDON · TORONTO · SYDNEY · AUCKLAND · JOHANNESBURG

TRANSWORLD PUBLISHERS
61–63 Uxbridge Road, London W5 5SA
A Random House Group Company
www.transworldbooks.co.uk

First published in the United States
in 2013 by Parallax Press
a publishing division of Unified Buddhist Church

First published in Great Britain
in 2014 by Bantam Press
an imprint of Transworld Publishers

A CIP catalogue record for this book
is available from the British Library.

ISBN 9780593073988

Addresses for Random House Group Ltd companies outside the UK
can be found at: www.randomhouse.co.uk
The Random House Group Ltd Reg. No. 954009

The Random House Group Limited supports The Forest Stewardship
Council® (FSC®), the leading international forest-certification organisation.
Our books carrying the FSC label are printed on FSC®-certified paper.
FSC is the only forest-certification scheme supported by the leading
environmental organisations, including Greenpeace. Our
paper procurement policy can be found at
www.randomhouse.co.uk/environment

Typeset in 10/18 pt Cassia Light
Printed and bound in Great Britain by Clays Ltd, St Ives plc

46810975

Contents

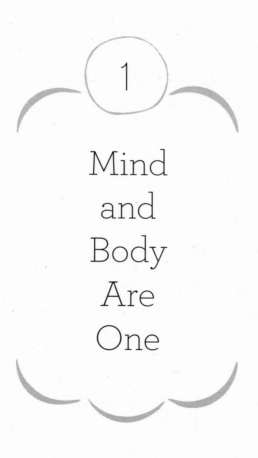

1

Mind and Body Are One

Why do we care about bringing body and mind together? Can't we just continue as we are? The way we're carrying on is making many of us sick. We're sick in our minds and in our bodies. Our planet is sick as well. Reuniting body and mind, which have become alienated from each other, reunites us with ourselves. Once we have come home to ourselves, we can be fully present for ourselves, fully present for others, and fully present for the planet.

If you are sad, anxious, or lonely, you may think you need to fix or change something in your mind. If your shoulders are tight, if your back aches, you may think you just need a doctor to help fix that area of your body. But the key to happiness is being fully integrated in body and mind. Much of our suffering comes from an unnecessary division of mind versus matter. We think that there's something wrong with our minds or something wrong with our bodies, and that we need to fix or heal that one, separate thing. But it's impossible to remove mind from body or body from mind. They are two manifestations of the same thing.

There are those who say that our mind is made of matter—the brain and the nervous system. That's a materialist view. There is mind, consciousness, intelligence, knowledge in every cell of our bodies. Each cell is a living reality with its own knowledge, its own mind. If you take consciousness out of a cell, the cell will die. If you take consciousness away from our bodies, they will be lifeless.

When we look into the heart of a flower, we can see that the flower isn't only matter; consciousness is present. When you plant a seed, it sprouts and becomes a plant. It's alive. There is mind inside. We can't even say that a speck of dust is only matter. Scientists have discovered that atoms and electrons are very intelligent; they're both matter and mind.

When we go walking outside in nature, we know that the Earth is not only made of earth. The Earth is also water, air, and fire. If we were to remove the elements of water, air, and fire from our planet, it would no longer be the Earth. In the past we believed that the Earth was the center of the cosmos. Now we know that the Earth isn't the center of the cosmos. In fact, anything and everything can be the center of the cosmos; a pebble, a squirrel, a piece of dust can be the center of the cosmos, because the one contains the all. This wisdom of nondiscrimination is the wisdom that doesn't divide things in two. It's sometimes called the wisdom of nonduality, *advaita jñana.*

There are scientists who are still caught in the idea that the mind is within us and that the world we study and observe is outside us. They believe that the subject of cognition is our mind and that its object is the world. As long as we follow this division between subject and object, mind and matter, we won't be able to touch the true nature of things. We will feel alienated. When we reconnect with our own bodies, and with our relationship to the world around us, happiness becomes possible.

Bringing Body and Mind Together

Breathing in, I'm aware of my whole body.
Breathing out, I'm aware of my whole body.

As you breathe in, you can connect with your body. Bring your mind home to your body and remember that you have a body. Very often we're carried far away by our thinking; we're caught by sorrow and regret concerning the past, by fear and anxiety concerning the future, or by our emotions or projects in the present. Our mind is not with our body. We're in a state of dispersion. Dispersion is the opposite of concentration. When you're truly here and concentrated, you can get in touch deeply with the wonders that are inside you and all around you. The sun, the moon, the stars, the trees, the river, the hills, and your body are all wonders that become available to you when you become fully present.

Practice: Coming Home to Your Body

If we know how to breathe mindfully, every breath will bring us happiness. People with asthma know how to appreciate the happiness of being able to breathe normally, and they can savor each breath. If our lungs are healthy and our noses aren't blocked, we can breathe easily. Not to enjoy that ease is like a wasted opportunity. With the practice of mindfulness, every breath brings happiness. Mindfulness can make every moment of our daily life peaceful, clear, and loving.

When we breathe in, we might breathe in such a way that joy is possible during the time of breathing in. The in-breath may last three or four seconds. If we know how to breathe in properly, we can generate the energy of joy just like that. When we breathe out, we can generate the energy of happiness for ourselves, as well as for others around us who benefit from our energy.

When we first begin to practice cultivating awareness, we give ourselves instructions in how to sit, breathe, and walk so that we can generate the energy of peace, happiness, and joy. Once we've received this teaching, we have to apply it in our daily lives. "Breathing in, I feel joy" is not autosuggestion or wishful thinking; it's a practice.

Coming home to the body is a strong practice. There may be pain, disharmony, suffering, or a lack of peace in the body. That's why we start by practicing mindfulness of the breath, so that we can recover ourselves and come home with strength and energy.

With the energy of mindful breathing, you come home to your body in order to make peace with it. By practicing mindful breathing, you generate harmony and solidity. Then you're in a position to go home to your whole body, in order to help your body. It's possible to continue mindful breathing while you embrace your body.

Breathing in, I'm aware of my whole body.
Breathing out, I recognize and embrace my whole body.

Your entire body becomes the object of your mindfulness. The subject of mindfulness is your mindful breathing. At first your breath is like an empty truck traveling along the highway, not transporting anything. But when you become aware of your breath and your body, your breath is like a truck that's carrying merchandise. That merchandise is insight. Mindful breathing embraces the whole body. It's very important to come home to your body, to recognize it, take care of it, and make peace with it.

The land of the present moment is available only in the here and the now. If you find yourself in the present moment, it means your mind and body are together. When you practice breathing in mindfully, you bring your mind home to your body and you find yourself in the land of the present moment. Mindfulness is the energy that helps the body and the mind come together. When body and mind are together, you are established in the present moment, in the kingdom, in the here and the now.

The opposite of mindfulness is forgetfulness. Our body may be there but our mind is somewhere else. Our mind may be caught in sorrow or regret concerning the past. Our mind may be caught in fear or uncertainty about the future. Or it may be caught in our anger or our projects. When we begin to breathe in mindfully, we can, in two or three seconds, bring our mind home to our body. Breathing in like that, mindfully, we release the past, we release the future, we release our projects, and we become free. That freedom allows us to get in touch with the wonders of life. It doesn't take a long time. A few seconds will do.

We breathe in and bring our attention to our in-breath; we release everything and we get a lot of freedom. With that kind of freedom, we can make better decisions. Our thoughts and our decisions are not skewed by our anger, our fear, our sorrow, or our regret. There will be a variety of options we can choose from. Our perspective will have become broader. When you come home to the here and the now with the practice of mindful breathing or mindful walking, you can recognize the many conditions of happiness that are already available. Mindfulness helps you to recognize that there are more than enough conditions to be happy right here and now. When you are in touch with these conditions, joy and happiness are possible right away.

2

The
Four
Qualities
of
Happiness

The practice of harmonizing body and mind brings more peace, clarity, compassion, and courage into our daily lives. With these four qualities, we can have enough happiness to be able to help others.

People tend to think of happiness in terms of having plenty of fame, power, wealth, and sensual pleasures. But we know that craving these objects can bring a lot of suffering. So we need to have a very different understanding of happiness. If we cultivate peace in ourselves, then clarity, compassion, and courage will come.

If you don't have compassion, you can't be a happy person. A person without compassion is someone who's utterly alone, who can't truly get in touch with another living being. With enough compassion you have the courage to liberate yourself and help liberate other people. That's true happiness, the kind of happiness that every one of us needs.

Peace

The first thing we need to do is to help our breathing become more peaceful and calm. With the intervention of mindfulness, our breath becomes more regular and harmonious. When we follow the course of our breath as we breathe in, our breathing naturally becomes deeper, slower, and more pleasant. We only need half a minute of mindful breathing to notice an improvement in the quality of our breathing. Our breath has become more peaceful and harmonious. This is the basis for bringing peace to our body, our feelings, our mind, and our perceptions.

Clarity

We often feel overwhelmed or confused. We don't think clearly. Our speech and actions in such moments may create suffering for ourselves and for the people around us. When we have more peace in ourselves, we begin to see things more clearly. Without peace, clarity isn't possible. Clarity helps remove wrong perceptions. When you have enough clarity, you see things as they really are, and what you do and say won't create suffering for you or for other people. Seeing things more clearly, you begin to have compassion, and anger and jealousy fade away. You begin to have understanding, and you don't want to blame or punish yourself or the other person anymore. You accept yourself as you are, you accept others as they are, and you look at yourself and others with the eyes of compassion.

Compassion

Compassion is the third quality we can cultivate through the practice. We are made of body and mind. Both body and mind are energy. We know now that matter is energy and energy is matter. Although we don't perform any physical movements while sitting in meditation, our body can actively radiate the energy of peace and compassion. Our body isn't just matter; it's energy. Our mind is also energy.

There are wholesome and unwholesome energies. Mind energy can be powerful. The energy of hate, fear, anger, or despair can be very strong and destructive. While sitting or walking in awareness, we don't generate these energies. Instead we generate the energies of mindfulness, peace, and compassion. When we know how to get in touch with the suffering inside us and the suffering in the world, the energy of compassion is born in us. That is the energy that can heal and transform.

Courage

With great compassion in you, you have the capacity to act with courage. You have enough courage to cut through habits of craving, anger, and so on. If you don't have enough compassion for yourself and others, you won't have the courage you need to cut off the afflictions that have been making you suffer.

Practice: Four Steps to Ending Alienation

To end the sense of separation and alienation and to revive peace, joy, and well-being in body and mind, return to your breath and get in touch with your body. It's through the door of the breath that you come home to the body. When you're in touch with the body, you're one with the body, and you know how to look after the body. When you're in touch with the body like that, you then have the chance to get in touch with the mind.

Not only are we often out of touch with our unpleasant feelings, we also frequently can't even be in touch with the pleasant feelings that exist within us. There are pleasant feelings, but we're losing ourselves in thinking and despair, and we can't recognize the pleasant feelings. We're also not able to be in touch with neutral feelings. Neutral feelings can become positive feelings once we become aware of them.

The method of the Buddha is very scientific. To help us end our alienation from others and ourselves, we first need to return to our bodies, to be in touch with our bodies, to resolve the things that are out of balance, and to reconcile with our bodies.

For a long time we've been oppressing our bodies. We think we love our body, but the truth is we've abandoned our body. Most people breathe and don't know that they're breathing. They need someone to teach them to breathe and to be in touch with their breathing.

Stopping and Calming the Body

One term for our body is "the body formation," *kaya samskara.* *Samskara* means formation, a composite phenomenon. A flower is a formation; it's composed of many different elements such as air, water, clouds, sunshine, and earth. These elements come together and make a formation. Our body is composed of different elements, like mother, father, teachers, earth, water, fire, and air. Our body is a composed thing, a formation.

There are three parts to beginning meditation. The first part is stopping. We stop all the thinking and bring our mind back to our body. The second aspect is calming down, calming our body formation. The third is concentrating and looking deeply.

Breathing in, I am aware of my whole body.
Breathing out, I am aware of my whole body.

Breathing in, I calm my body.
Breathing out, I calm my body.

My body is suffering. My body has been abandoned. I've neglected my body and treated it poorly. Now I return to my body and I say, "I'm sorry, my dear body. I will look after you from now on." I look after my body carefully. First of all, I breathe in and out in such a way that when I breathe, my body calms down.

The in-breath and out-breath have the function of helping my body to calm down. We calm the body formation by breathing with awareness. I bring peace back into my body. When my body is abandoned, there's pain, there's tension, and there's no peace. But if I breathe correctly, mindfully, the breath can help to ease the tension and pain. Calming the breath will calm the body and reduce the suffering. That's what is meant by calming the body.

Breathing in, I calm my body.
Breathing out, I bring peace into my body.

Being Aware of the Body

We breathe mindfully to be aware of the body formation.

Breathing in, I'm aware that I have a body.
Breathing out, I know my body is there.

That is already awakening. Don't look for enlightenment somewhere else.

During the many hours we spend at work, we forget that we have a body. Once we've lost ourselves, we've lost everything. In the body there's tension. Now we come back and we breathe in and out in such a way as to remove the tension and bring peace to the body.

Breathing in, I bring peace to my body.
Breathing out, I release the tension.

If we have some feelings that are painful or uncomfortable, then we have to breathe in order to calm the breathing and bring that calming into the feelings. Each breath we take, each step we make can bring peace to our body and to our feelings.

Calming the Mind

The mind is also a formation, a samskara. Perceptions, feelings, emotions—they are all formations. When we breathe, we make these mental formations calm. This is called calming the mental formation.

Breathing in, I calm my mind.
Breathing out, I calm my feelings, my emotions.

Each of us can learn how to breathe in such a way as to calm the body and our strong mental formations, and bring peace into body and mind. If we know how to breathe, we can ease our inner turmoil.

When our mind and our body have calmed down, we begin to see more clearly. Instead of being lost, ill, alienated, we have clarity, we have vision. We don't make nearly as many mistakes. Peace is followed by tranquility and clarity. When we see our anger and sadness clearly, a kind of miracle can happen and we're no longer angry or sad. We begin to feel compassion. Clarity is brought about by peace of body and mind. That brings happiness and love. Without love, it's not possible to feel truly happy.

3

Full-Body
Meditation

The only way to gain genuine peace, clarity, compassion, and courage is through mindful awareness. Mindful awareness is full attention, with the whole body and mind, to what is happening in the present moment. When body and mind come together in awareness, fully established in the here and the now, we are free and we can live every moment of our daily lives deeply and happily.

There are three elements of awareness we need to bring together to be fully present. The first is the breath, the second is the body, and the third is the mind. Mindful awareness can happen throughout the day, whatever we are doing. One way to practice and gain the skill and habit of being aware is through full-body meditation. Full-body meditation can be done either while sitting or walking. Mind, body, and breath are together. Harmonizing these three elements, we become whole. We show up for ourselves, for our loved ones, for the world, and for life.

The practice of full-body meditation begins with the breath. You can say to yourself silently:

Breathing in, I know I'm breathing in.
Breathing out, I know I'm breathing out.

In just two or three seconds of conscious breathing you can bring your mind home to your body.

In daily life, you may often feel dispersed. Your body is in one place, ignored, your breath is ignored, and your mind is wandering. But as soon as you pay attention to your breath and breathe in, then all three elements come together in just a few seconds. You pull yourself together, and there you are in the here and the now.

A Nonviolent Response

Perhaps anger, fear, or restlessness has taken root in your mind. Don't be too eager to control your breath or your feelings. Allow them to be themselves. This is the most nonviolent way of taking care of our strong emotions. Take time just to sit and breathe, even for just five minutes.

Don't force your breathing. Simply become aware of your in-breath and out-breath. If your in-breath is short, allow it to be short. If your out-breath isn't peaceful, just allow it to be like that. With awareness, your in-breath and out-breath will naturally begin to flow more easily.

When you breathe in, pay attention only to your in-breath.

Don't force or fight with your breathing. Allow it to be the way it is. Your breathing will naturally become calmer, deeper, and more harmonious by itself; that's the effect of mindfulness. Just continue to breathe and to smile gently to your breathing. In a few minutes you'll see that the quality of your breathing has increased by itself, and that will have an influence right away on your body and on your mind. Peace and calm are contagious.

When we're upset, perhaps we think, "I should meditate" or "I should practice mindful breathing." But mindfulness practices are not something we have to do. They are something we get to do. The practices of mindful breathing, mindful sitting, and mindful walking exist only to help us to cultivate more peace in ourselves and become more fully present. Every moment is an opportunity for us to do this.

Mindful Body and Embodied Mind

When you sit and breathe mindfully, body and mind easily and naturally come back together. You don't have to strain. Bringing the body and mind together, you have a mindful body and an embodied mind. A mindful body is a body with awareness. The embodied mind is the mind that is fully present in the body. It's like software and hardware. If your software and hardware aren't communicating with each other, you can't do anything.

Following your breathing and bringing your mind back to

your body allows you to be here in the present moment. Let go of everything so you can have freedom, so you can be in touch with the wonders of the universe. We see that all the stars are in us; the galaxy is in us. Sitting like that is a miracle. We embrace limitless space and time. It's possible to sit like that for five, ten, fifteen, or thirty minutes. We enjoy every moment. How many people in the world can sit like that, or have the chance to learn how to sit like that? We have many opportunities to sit mindfully during the day.

Mindful Walking

Walking meditation is always full-body meditation. It can't be done any other way. We combine our breathing with our steps. While we're breathing in, we may take two, three, or four steps. As we breathe out, we may want to take a few more steps. For example, when we're breathing in, if we take two steps, then when breathing out, we may take three steps. If when breathing in we take three steps, then when breathing out we might take four or five steps. If when breathing in we take five steps, while breathing out we may take eight steps. Let the rhythm of your breathing and walking be natural, whatever fits your own breath.

We can use words when we do walking meditation. As we breathe in and take two or three steps, we can say, "I have arrived."

As we breathe out, we can say, "I am home." With every step, we really arrive; we're really at home. We don't wander around in the past or the future. We feel at ease, peaceful, and secure when we are fully in the present moment. We don't have to run after anything else anymore. Anyone who enjoys walking or sitting can feel satisfied. We have nothing else to look for, nothing more to long for.

If your in-breath is three steps and your out-breath is five steps, you can say, "I have arrived. I have really arrived. With every step, I return to my source." We can use whatever sentences we like. There are many wonderful sentences we can use. When we want to switch, we can find another. Each step is returning to the source.

I have arrived.
I am home.

Walking on the Earth

When we do walking meditation, we don't walk with our body alone, because our body and mind are united. That's why it's best if we don't talk when we walk. Every step is in noble silence. When we step on the Earth, we don't see the Earth as mere matter. To look at the Earth only as matter is incorrect; that's being caught in materialism. But on the other hand to see the Earth as just consciousness, as philosopher George Berkeley did, is too idealistic. Materialism is one extreme and idealism is another extreme. Both are based on the theory that mind and matter are two different things; either there is only mind or only matter.

When we look deeply into the body, we see that the body is not only matter. There is intelligence in it. Every cell in our bodies—and there are trillions of cells—has its intelligence and its very deep understanding. So it's not correct to say our bodies are only matter. Without consciousness there would be no life in the body.

When we look at something in the natural world—at a blade of grass or a tree—we see that it has its knowledge. When we look into a seed of corn, we see that it's more than just matter. When we sow a seed in the Earth, the seed knows how to grow into a plant, produce flowers, and bear fruit. So to say that maize is only matter is wrong. When we look at the Earth, we see that the Earth is a wondrous reality. It has its knowledge, just as each cell has its knowledge. The planet Earth can give birth to life and nourish life. If you say our planet Earth is just a lump of matter, that's incorrect. With advaita jñana, the wisdom of nonduality, we see our planet is not just an inanimate mass of minerals. It has intelligence and creativity. This planet has produced wonderful things, so many species. The human species is just one of the many species that this planet Earth has produced.

When we do walking meditation, we use our wisdom of nonduality. We see that we're not stepping on mere matter. We see that we're touching our own Mother Earth, a wonderful reality. She doesn't have to be a human being to be a mother. She is the mother of us all, with the capacity to carry, birth, nourish, and heal us.

When we're in ill health, we sometimes lose ourselves. We have to return to our mother, the Earth, to be healed again. Walking meditation is a wonderful practice that can help us to return and find healing from Mother Earth. The Earth is a bodhisattva with great virtues like solidity and patience. In the Kshitigarbha Sutra it says that Earth is "persevering, solid, and stores many things."

Every Step Is for Relaxation

When you walk from one place to another, as you walk be totally in the present moment. When you walk, take steps in a relaxed way, enjoying the beauty around you. Be totally with the present moment, with the spring rain, with the autumn leaves. Walk in a free and leisurely manner, and arrive home at every step. Taking steps and breathing in and out, you can say,

I arrive in the present moment.
I am home in the here and now.

When you walk relaxingly, happily, you are already practicing mindful awareness.

When you walk and others see that you radiate peace, happiness, and calm, you're a reminder for all of us. When we see you walking like that, we come back to ourselves and we walk in the same way as you. You contribute to generating the collective energy of mindfulness and peace that will nourish and transform us all. When we practice together, we give and we receive. We offer the energies of mindfulness, concentration, peace, and happiness and we receive these energies from others. The quality of collective practice is the basis of a practice community.

Your steps must bring you back to the present moment and to what is nourishing. You don't need to rush. There's nothing to rush for. Every step is for relaxing.

You wish to be successful in your practice. When you practice peace of mind, everyone wants you to be successful. You walk not only for yourself, but also for your parents who may never have had a chance to practice, for your ancestors, your teacher, your friends. In fact, you walk so that everyone will be happy. It looks like you're walking alone, but you're not alone. There are many people around who need your practice to be happy and relaxed.

Lying Down or Going to Sleep

As well as when you're sitting or walking, full-body meditation can be practiced when you're about to go to sleep. Lie down on your back. Instead of thinking of this and that, go back to your breathing and practice breathing in and breathing out. You may like to notice and say to yourself as you breathe in and out,

Joy while breathing;
happiness while resting.

If you concentrate on your in-breath and out-breath and allow joy and happiness to be generated, you'll likely find you can go to sleep peacefully.

Joy while breathing;
Joy is the breathing.

They are the same thing. Joy doesn't exist outside of the breathing. The breathing is joy itself. This is because the quality of breathing is so high; it's mindful breathing, the kind of breathing that brings harmony, calm, and joy. So the joy is the breathing. We're not using the breathing in order to bring joy. Joy becomes the breathing. The breathing becomes joy.

The word *bhavana* means cultivation. This describes how

we train ourselves in the practice of meditation. We're able to produce something that wasn't there before. It's like growing flowers, wheat, or corn. Bhavana means we bring something into existence. In English we use the word "practice." If we have a practice that is good, that is solid, we shouldn't be afraid of anything, because the practice helps us generate joy, happiness, peace, harmony, and reconciliation; and it helps us to handle pain, suffering, separation, and misunderstanding. With mindful awareness and the practice of full-body meditation, we can begin to know ourselves fully. There's no reason to be afraid.

Practice: Deep Relaxation

Give yourself at least twenty minutes. When you do deep relaxation in a group, one person can guide the exercise using the following cues or some variation of them. For deep relaxation on your own, you may like to record an exercise to follow as you practice. Deep relaxation can be done at home, at the office or anywhere, at least once a day, wherever you have the space to lie comfortably. If you can't lie down, you can sit in a chair.

Lie down on your back with your arms at your sides. Make yourself comfortable. Allow your body to relax. Be aware of the floor beneath you . . . and of the contact of your body with the floor. (Breathe.) Allow your body to sink into the floor. (Breathe.)

Become aware of your breathing, in and out. Be aware of your abdomen rising and falling as you breathe in and out. (Breathe.) Rising... falling... rising... falling. (Breathe.)

Breathing in, bring your awareness to your eyes. Breathing out, allow your eyes to relax. Allow your eyes to sink back into your head... letting go of the tension in all the tiny muscles around your eyes. Our eyes allow us to see a paradise of shapes and colors.... Allow your eyes to rest... sending love and gratitude to your eyes.... (Breathe.)

Breathing in, bring your awareness to your mouth. Breathing out, allow your mouth to relax. Release the tension around your mouth.... Your lips are the petals of a flower.... Let a gentle smile bloom on your lips.... Smiling releases the tension in the dozens of muscles in your face.... Feel the tension release in your cheeks ... your jaw... your throat.... (Breathe.)

Breathing in, bring your awareness to your shoulders. Breathing out, allow your shoulders to relax. Let them sink into the floor.... Let all the accumulated tension flow into the floor.... You carry so much with your shoulders ... now let them relax as you care for your shoulders. (Breathe.)

Breathing in, become aware of your arms. Breathing out, relax your arms. Let your arms sink into the floor . . . your upper arms . . . your elbows . . . your lower arms . . . your wrists . . . hands . . . fingers . . . all the tiny muscles. . . . Move your fingers a little if you need to, to help the muscles relax. (Breathe.)

Breathing in, bring your awareness to your heart. Breathing out, allow your heart to relax. (Breathe.) You have neglected your heart for a long time . . . in the way you work, eat, and manage anxiety and stress. (Breathe.) Your heart beats for you night and day. Embrace your heart with mindfulness and tenderness . . . reconciling and taking care of your heart. (Breathe.)

Breathing in, bring your awareness to your legs. Breathing out, allow your legs to relax. Release all the tension in your legs . . . your thighs . . . your knees . . . your calves . . . your ankles . . . your feet . . . your toes . . . all the tiny muscles in your toes. . . . You may want to move your toes a little to help them relax. . . . Send your love and care to your toes. (Breathe.)

Breathing in, breathing out . . . your whole body feels light . . . like a water lily floating on the water. . . . You have nowhere to go . . . nothing to do. . . . You are free as the cloud floating in the sky. (Breathe.)

Now you can listen to singing or music for a few minutes. (Breathe.)

Bring your awareness back to your breathing . . . to your abdomen rising and falling. (Breathe.)

Following your breathing, become aware of your arms and legs. . . . You may want to move them a little and stretch. (Breathe.)

When you feel ready, slowly sit up. (Breathe.)

When you are ready, slowly stand up.

4

Finding
Peace

Whether you're walking or sitting, the first thing to do for full-body meditation is to bring peace to your breath, your body, and your emotions. This may seem like a lot, but if you follow your breath, it can happen quite naturally. As soon as you sit down or begin your walk, bring your attention to your in-breath and out-breath. Your breathing may become peaceful in no time at all. It's important not to force your breathing. When your breath has become more peaceful, harmonious, and pleasant, you begin to enjoy breathing in and breathing out, and to benefit from the harmony and peace brought to you by the practice.

Making Our Bodies Peaceful

The next thing to do is to recognize your body. This is a very important practice, because many of us in our daily lives forget that we have a body. This exercise of going back to our body reminds us that each of us has a body that is our home. If you can get in touch with your body, then you can get in touch with life. "Breathing in, I'm aware of my body. Breathing out, I know my body is there."

When you're lost in your computer, you're not living in a real world. In Plum Village we like to download a bell that sounds every fifteen minutes on the computer. When you're working and you hear the bell, you go back to your in-breath and your out-breath. You breathe in and you recognize that you have a body. When you come back to your body, you touch life; you get in touch with everything inside and around you. Breathing in and out and being aware of your body helps release tension and brings peace into your body, and you feel how pleasant it is to be with the body.

As soon as our in-breath and out-breath have become more peaceful and pleasant, our body begins to benefit. In our body there may not be enough peace. There may be tension, stress, pain in our body, whether we're aware of it or not. There's suffering in our body when there's not enough peace. But as soon as our in-breath and out-breath begin to become more peaceful, that peace will be conveyed to our body.

All of us can learn to bring more peace into our bodies. Whether we're sitting, standing, walking, lying down, eating, or working, we can always practice mindful breathing to release the tension in our body and bring in more peace. We can say to ourselves,

Breathing in, I am aware of my body.
Breathing out, I release the tension in my body.

We bring the mind back to the body, we recognize the presence of the body, and we release any tension being held in the body. This brings peace to our body and it can be done in just a few minutes. Peace is something very concrete; there's a harmonious, pleasant feeling born from peace. With the practice of mindful breathing, it's possible to make your breathing and your body peaceful.

The Buddha advises that after becoming aware of the whole body, we can become aware of the four elements of water, fire, air, and earth within the body. Focus on each element and see if you can sense this element in your body. Up to 60 percent of the human body is water; the brain is composed of 70 percent water; 83 percent of our blood is water, which helps us digest our food. For fire, we can think of the heat and energy we can generate in our bodies to keep us warm and digest our food. Air is our life's breath. Earth is what we eat and digest, and the vitamins and minerals in our blood and bones. If there is balance among the four elements, then there is good health. Much of human illness comes from an imbalance between these four elements. Recognize the four elements within, and recognize the four elements all around you, to see the connection between the body and everything we normally think of as "outside" of the body.

Then we become aware of the positions of the body. While seated, you're aware that you're sitting. While walking, you're aware of the steps you make. Sitting meditation is first of all to be aware that we are in a sitting position. We can sit in a way that brings calmness, solidity, and well-being to our body. When walking, walk in a way that brings solidity, freedom, and pleasure for you while walking. Sitting, walking, standing, and lying down, you are mindful of each of these four basic positions of your body. That is the practice of mindfulness regarding the body. Then we become aware of every action of the body: getting up, bending down, putting on our coat—every gesture of your body should be followed and become the object of your mindfulness.

Peace in the Feelings

The peace we achieve by breathing attentively can benefit not only our body but also our feelings and perceptions. Mindfulness helps us get in touch with what's going on in our body, our feelings, and our perceptions. We make them the objects of our meditation. There are many wonderful things in us and around us. When we make them the objects of our mindfulness they can nourish and heal us. Every morning when we wake up, we can breathe in with awareness and get in touch with the wonders of life. Mindfulness allows us to be in touch with those wonderful nourishing things that bring healing, joy, and happiness. The first benefits of mindfulness are joy and happiness.

Calming Painful Feelings

Full-body meditation helps us become aware of each feeling as it arises, whether it's a pleasant feeling, an unpleasant feeling, a neutral feeling, or a mixed feeling. Before attending to painful feelings, we need to learn how to relate skillfully with the feelings that are not painful. We cultivate joy and happiness to nourish ourselves so we have the capacity and energy to take care of the painful feelings. Calming our breathing and our body and releasing tension can already bring a feeling of joy, a feeling of happiness.

Breathing in, I feel joy.
Breathing out, I smile to the joy in myself.

Breathing in, I feel happy.
Breathing out, I smile to the feeling of happiness in myself.

We don't always want to go directly to the painful feeling. It's better to nourish ourselves with feelings of joy and happiness first. When a person needs to undergo surgery, usually the surgeon will recommend that the patient get plenty of rest ahead of time in order to be in the strongest possible state to bear the difficulties of surgery.

If you have a painful feeling, mindfulness will help you recognize it. With the release of tension in your body you can reduce the amount of pain in your body and also in your feelings. A painful feeling may have a cause in the body or in the perceptions. Fear and anger usually come from wrong perceptions. If you know how to recognize your feeling and embrace it tenderly with your mindful breathing, you can help to calm it down.

Breathing in, I'm aware of a painful feeling.
Breathing out, I calm my painful feeling.

You bring in peace. This is the cultivation of peace through the practice of mindful breathing and mindful sitting.

You can also cultivate peace through the practice of mindful walking. We can walk to release the tension in our bodies and also to be in touch with the Earth. Walking mindfully helps us be aware that to be able to touch the Earth, our mother, is a great happiness and one we can enjoy any time we like. We should know how to generate a pleasant feeling for ourselves with mindfulness. We should be able to help another person do it too. It's always possible to bring in a pleasant feeling.

When you're in touch with a painful feeling, mindfulness can help you to embrace, soothe, and calm that pain. Mindfulness puts you in touch with the positive things, and it also brings awareness of the things that are painful.

You may have anger. Instead of letting that anger ravage your mind and body, you can breathe mindfully, come back to your body, and embrace this difficult feeling with the energy of mindfulness.

Breathing in, I know that anger is in me.
Breathing out, I embrace my anger.

Right away there will be a difference. Without mindfulness, there's just the energy of anger, which can push us to say and do things that can cause damage. But when we can bring up a second energy, the energy of mindfulness, it recognizes, embraces, and soothes the energy of anger.

When anger comes up, become aware of your breathing and generate the energy of mindfulness. The energy of anger is still there, but now the energy of mindfulness is also there, recognizing and embracing the anger. "My little anger, I am here for you; I'm going to take good care of you." In that moment there are two energies operating: the suffering, and the mindfulness that recognizes and embraces the suffering. Practicing like this, you can obtain relief very quickly.

When a mother hears her baby cry, she goes into the baby's room, picks up the baby, and embraces the baby with a lot of tenderness. When that tenderness begins to penetrate into the body of the baby, the baby suffers less right away, even before the mother has found out what's wrong. It's the same with your suffering. The suffering is your baby and you are the mother. "Hello, my little anger. I am here. I'm always here for you." With the practice of conscious breathing, you generate the energy of mindfulness that recognizes and tenderly embraces the pain in you. Relief comes right away. That is the second function of mindfulness. It's an art we can all learn.

With mindfulness, we can nourish and heal ourselves with positive things, and we can embrace and relieve suffering. When you can keep that mindfulness alive, then concentration is there. Concentration is born from mindfulness. When you maintain mindfulness, concentration arises. With concentration you're able to look deeply into what is there. You can make a breakthrough into reality. Insight is born from mindfulness and concentration.

Practice: The Sixteen Exercises of Mindful Breathing

In the Sutra on the Full Awareness of Breathing, the Buddha proposed sixteen exercises of mindful breathing. We've seen already that our body and mind inter-are. The first four exercises of mindful breathing are for us to bring the mind back to the body and take care of the body. The next four exercises are to contemplate and take care of the feelings. The third set of four is to contemplate our mind, which means our mental formations. The last set of four is to help us correct our perceptions by looking into the true nature of things so reality can reveal itself to us. This kind of insight can liberate us from ignorance, suffering, and fear.

1. AWARENESS OF BREATHING

The first exercise is to be aware of your in-breath and out-breath. As you breathe in, bring your attention to your in-breath. Focus your attention only on your in-breath and release everything else. You release the past, the future, your projects, and you are free. Just by breathing in, you are free, because in that moment you are not your sorrow, your fear, or your regret. You are only your in-breath.

Breathing in, I know I'm breathing in.
Breathing out, I know I'm breathing out.

Although the exercise is very simple, the result can be great. We may get free just by focusing our attention on our in-breath and out-breath.

When we wake up each morning, we have the opportunity to return to our body. Breathing in, we recognize there is an in-breath.

Breathing in, I know that this is an in-breath.
Breathing out, I know that this is an out-breath.

That is enlightenment. You don't have to practice eight years to be enlightened. Normally we don't know we're breathing in; we just breathe in. Now, we breathe in, we put our mind into it, and we know we're breathing in. We recognize "I'm breathing in." Breathing in makes us feel alive. To be alive is something wonderful.

We see this as the ABC, or basis, of mindfulness practice. But it's not just the ABC, because on the very first day of practice, knowing that there's an in-breath or an out-breath happening, you're already enlightened. Breathing in and breathing out in awareness can be very enjoyable.

So in this exercise we identify the in-breath as an in-breath and the out-breath as an out-breath. The effect can be very deep, because when you pay attention to your in-breath and go home to your body, you suddenly get the insight: "I have a body." When mind and body are together, you are truly in the here and now to live your life. Please don't underestimate this easy exercise. Even if you've practiced mindful breathing for ten or twenty years, this remains a very wonderful practice, and you continue to get more and more benefit from it.

2. FOLLOWING THE BREATH

The second exercise of mindful breathing is,

> *Breathing in, I follow my in-breath*
> *from the beginning to the end.*
> *Breathing out, I follow my out-breath*
> *from the beginning to the end.*

During the time of breathing in and out, you cultivate not only mindfulness, but also concentration.

There's no interruption in your attention during the time of the in-breath and out-breath. By focusing your mind entirely on your in-breath and out-breath, you cultivate concentration. The object of your concentration is your in-breath. Not a millisecond is lost; you are entirely with your in-breath, and you dwell very solidly in your in-breath. There's no more thinking, no more past, no more future; you're really enjoying your in-breath. While you're breathing in, many insights may come to you, like, "Breathing in—I'm alive!" You can celebrate the miracle of being alive just by breathing in. That is happiness already. You don't have to go looking for happiness elsewhere. Just sit and breathe in and enjoy the fact that you are alive. It's a pleasure to follow your in-breath and out-breath all the way through and develop concentration. You don't have to suffer during the practice.

When you focus your attention on your breath, you will find out very quickly that you are a living reality, present here and now, sitting on this beautiful planet Earth. Around you there are trees, sunshine, and blue sky. Mindfulness and concentration put you in touch with the wonders of life and allow you to treasure and value these things.

When you practice mindful breathing while walking, you see that it's a wonder to be alive and making steps on this beautiful planet; happiness comes right away. Happiness isn't made of money, fame, and power, but of mindfulness of breathing. By following your breath and enjoying it all the way through, you cultivate more concentration, because mindfulness and concentration are of the same essential nature, like water and ice. Where there's mindfulness and concentration, there's also insight. Mindfulness carries concentration and insight within it.

Breathing in, you touch the fact that you're alive, that your lungs are still healthy and you can breathe in freely—that is already insight. There are people who breathe in who don't know they're breathing in. They don't know that they're alive and that there are wonders of life in and around them; so there can be no insight. But you who breathe mindfully, you know that you're alive, that life is a miracle, that you're living that miracle in the here and the now. That is insight already. You don't have to practice eight years or twenty years in order to have insight. A few seconds of mindfulness and concentration can already bring you some insight. It is these three energies of mindfulness, concentration, and insight that can create joy and happiness. "Breathing in, I feel joy" isn't autosuggestion. It's what you actually experience.

With the three energies of mindfulness, concentration, and insight we can easily bring joy and peace into every moment of our daily lives.

3. AWARE OF BODY

The third exercise is to become aware of our body.

Breathing in, I'm aware of my whole body.
Breathing out, I'm aware of my whole body.

We reconnect with our body every time we remember our body is there. When body and mind are together, we are truly present in the here and the now and we can live every moment of daily life deeply. "Breathing in, I'm aware that I have a body." That is an awakening.

We reconcile with our body, we become our body, and we stop the alienation and separation of body and mind from each other. When we return to our body, we become aware of the suffering, the heaviness, and suppression in our body. We know that we have to be kind to our body and give it an opportunity to relax.

Breathing in, I relax my body and mind.
Breathing out, I calm my body and mind.

Stopping comes first; calming is second. It's wonderful to stop. It's even more wonderful to calm down. Suffering begins to lessen.

With mindful breathing you can go back to your body and touch the wonder that is the body. If we know how to be in touch with our body and connect with our body, we will connect with Mother Earth and the whole cosmos. We begin with our in-breath. With our in-breath, we go home to our body. Going home to our body, we go home to Mother Earth, and we touch the whole cosmos.

When mind and body are together, we establish ourselves in the here and the now and we are truly alive. When mind and body are apart, we're not really there. Breathing in to bring mind and body together, that is the moment when we are truly alive. When we can touch the wonders of life inside and around us; that is life.

When we're with our body, not only do we touch the wonder of our bodies, but we may realize that there is something in our bodies that needs to be transformed, like tension and pain. Living in forgetfulness, we've allowed the tension and pain to accumulate in our bodies. We have a lot of stress every day. Modern life causes tension and stress to accumulate in our bodies.

4. RELEASING TENSION IN THE BODY

Being with your body, you may notice that it holds tension, pain, and stress. You would like to do something to release the tension and reduce the pain in your body. While breathing in and breathing out, you just allow the tension in your body to be released. That is the practice of deep relaxation.

Breathing in, I calm my body.
Breathing out, I release the tension in my body.

We can do this while sitting, standing, walking, or lying down. We can also do it when we drive our car or cook our breakfast. We don't have to set aside a special time to do these things.

Whatever the position of the body, whether you're lying, standing, sitting, or walking, you can always release the tension. Sitting on the bus, you can practice breathing and release the tension. Walking to the classroom, the workplace, or the meditation hall, you can allow the tension to be released with each step. You walk as a free person. You enjoy every step you make. You're not in a hurry anymore. Walk wth ease, releasing the tension in the body with each step. This is the way to walk every time you need to move from one place to another.

We don't need to set aside a special time to practice. We can practice all day long and get the benefit of practice right away. Driving the car, taking a shower, cooking breakfast, we can enjoy doing those things. We shouldn't say, "I have no time to practice." We have plenty of time. When you practice and you get relaxation and joy, it benefits everyone around you. To practice mindful breathing is an act of love. You become an instrument of peace and joy, and you can help others.

Although these four exercises are for helping us get in touch with our body, we see that the mind is already deeply involved. Without the mind, we cannot take care of our body, and without the body, we cannot take care of our mind. The mind is taking care of the body and the body is supporting the mind; they're not enemies.

5. FEELINGS

With the fifth exercise we come to the realm of the feelings. The first feeling we need to be in touch with is our joy. When we wake up to the fact that we have a body, that we have life, and that we can be in touch with the wonders of life, there arises the joy of being alive. So it can be very natural and easy to produce a feeling of joy.

Breathing in, I feel joy.
Breathing out, I feel joy.

We lose ourselves in our work, in our worries, and we can't see the wonders of life. Now we're returning and we're in touch with the clear air, the cup of tea, the flowers and grass, with the wonderful planet Earth. We see that we have two eyes and two ears that allow us to be in touch with those wonders. Joy comes easily.

6. HAPPINESS

The sixth exercise is to produce a feeling of happiness. Happiness is possible here and now. You need only to breathe in for a few seconds and you become enlightened about the fact that it's possible to be happy right away. It helps to remind us that mindfulness and concentration are sources of happiness. Many people believe that more wealth, more power, more fame will make them happy. But those of us who practice mindfulness know that mindfulness is a source of happiness. Joy and happiness differ a little in that joy still contains some amount of excitement.

Breathing in, I feel happy.
Breathing out, I feel happy.

If we've mastered the first four exercises, it becomes very easy, because when we breathe in and out, bring our mind back to our body, and release the tension in our body, then we find ourselves established in the here and the now and we're in a position to recognize that we have more conditions than we need to be happy. There are so many wonders of life.

There's a belief that we don't have enough conditions of happiness. There's a tendency to run into the future and look for more conditions of happiness. The French have a song with the title "What Are We Waiting for to Be Happy?" "Breathing in, I'm aware of the feeling of happiness" is not imagination or wishful thinking, because when we return to ourselves, we can be in touch with the wonders of life. Then we will have joy and happiness. This is the teaching and practice of the Buddha. We don't look for the Buddha in his body, we look for the Buddha in his teachings. The Buddha is continued by the teachings and the practice. In this way we can be in touch with the Buddha in the present moment.

7. RECOGNIZING PAINFUL FEELINGS

When a painful feeling or emotion arises, recognize and embrace it tenderly without the desire to suppress it.

Breathing in, I'm aware of a painful feeling in me.
Breathing out, I'm aware of a painful feeling in me.

This is the practice of simple recognition of the painful feeling that is arising. There is the energy of pain, but there is also the energy of mindfulness that is embracing the pain. Those who don't know how to practice allow the pain to overwhelm them or they try to run away from the pain by bringing in something else to cover up the painful feeling. It may be eating something, listening to music; doing anything not to be confronted with the suffering inside. The market provides us with everything we can use to cover up the suffering inside. By consuming like this, we allow the suffering inside to grow more. We have to be in touch with our pain in order to have an opportunity to heal the pain.

We suffer, we are sick—that's why we practice meditation, to get better, to be free of suffering. We get in touch with joy and happiness, as well as our suffering and pain. Those of us who know the practice use the energy of mindfulness to recognize and tenderly embrace the energy of pain. Bringing our mind back to our body and cultivating joy and happiness gives us the strength we need to encounter and embrace our painful feelings. We aren't running away or covering up anymore. Recognizing and embracing the painful feeling puts an end to the alienation between body and mind.

8. RELIEVING A PAINFUL FEELING

When we know how to tenderly embrace our pain, we can already get some relief just by doing so. That is the practice of the eighth exercise of mindful breathing, relieving the pain and bringing relief to a painful feeling or emotion.

Breathing in, I embrace my painful feeling.
Breathing out, I calm my painful feeling.

Every time we notice that a painful feeling or emotion is coming up, we always come back to our mindful breathing and generate the energy of mindfulness to recognize and embrace the pain, in the same way that a loving mother recognizes the suffering of her child and embraces the child lovingly in her arms.

With these four exercises for the feelings, we know how to handle happiness and pain. If we know how to handle happiness, we are able to nourish it and make it last. We can nourish our love, peace, and happiness and keep them there for a long time. When there's pain, we're not afraid because we know how to handle it, how to get relief, and how to transform the pain into something else, like greater understanding.

In the beginning we may not know where our suffering has come from, but because we're able to recognize and hold it tenderly, we suffer less already. Some relief is obtained. If we continue with mindfulness and concentration, we'll soon discover the nature and the roots of our pain and suffering. If you're depressed, you may not know why that depression has come. It's as though it's come from out of the blue. But everything has its source, its roots. If you know how to generate the energy of mindfulness and concentration, recognize your depression, and embrace it, you'll suffer less already. With mindfulness you can concentrate on looking into the nature of your depression, and you will find out how and from where that depression has come.

9. RECOGNIZING MENTAL FORMATIONS

With the next exercise of mindful breathing, we come to the realm of the mind. This ninth exercise is to recognize any thoughts or mental formations when they arise.

Breathing in, I'm aware of my mind.
Breathing out, I'm aware of my mind.

In Buddhism, there are fifty-one categories of mental formations. There are beneficial mental formations like joy, happiness, brotherhood, tolerance, mindfulness, concentration, understanding, and love. There are also negative mental formations like anger, fear, despair, and jealousy. All these mental formations are in our consciousness in the form of seeds. Every time one of them manifests as energy, we want to have enough awareness to recognize them. It's helpful if you know about their characteristics so that when each of them comes up, you can recognize it and call it by its true name.

Hello there, my mental formation.
Your name is jealousy.
I know you.
I will take good care of you.

That is the ninth exercise of mindful breathing. You sit on the bank of the river of mental formations and recognize any mental formation that arises.

10. GLADDENING THE MIND

The tenth exercise is to make our mental landscape beautiful.

Breathing in, I make my mind happy.
Breathing out, I make my mind happy.

We know that there are good mental formations down in the depths of our consciousness, like love, forgiveness, joy, and understanding. We should be able in our daily life to nourish them and give them a chance to manifest as beautiful mental formations. Whenever the mental formation of compassion or joy arises, we feel wonderful. We have many good mental formations like this in our consciousness and we should give them a chance to manifest as often as possible.

We know that our partner, our loved one, also has good things inside, and we may like to say or do something to help these good things to come up and make her happy. You don't want to water the seeds of anger, fear, and jealousy in her. You only want to water the seeds of joy, happiness, and compassion in yourself and in her. This is called the practice of selective watering. It's a practice known in Buddhism as Right Diligence or Right Effort. This practice strengthens our minds so that when we want to embrace and look into our negative mental formations, we're able to do so with more clarity and solidity.

11. CONCENTRATION

The eleventh exercise is to practice concentrating our mind. To meditate means to be present and to concentrate on the object of your meditation.

Breathing in, I concentrate my mind.
Breathing out, I concentrate my mind.

The object of your meditation may be your body, your anger, or your despair. It may be your happiness; it may be the kingdom of God or the Pure Land of the Buddha. During that time you only have one object, and you wholly concentrate your mind on that object. It's like a lens receiving rays of sunlight. The lens will concentrate the rays so they converge on one spot under the lens. If you hold a piece of paper in that spot, it will catch on fire. When you concentrate your mind at a single point, you may be able to make a breakthrough into the nature of the object of your meditation, and you get the kind of insight, the kind of view that will help to liberate you. The practice of concentration has the power to free you. The things that bind us, that don't allow us to be free, are our anger, craving, and delusion.

12. LIBERATION

We want to be liberated from such things as attachment, anger, violence, and delusion because these things are the cause of our suffering.

> Breathing in, I liberate my mind.
> Breathing out, I liberate my mind.

In terms of salvation, what we want to be saved from is our anger, fear, and delusion. Happiness is possible when we are liberated from these elements.

With the eighth exercise of mindful breathing, you're capable of getting some relief. With the eleventh and twelfth exercises you can liberate yourself entirely from the pain.

13. IMPERMANENCE

The last four exercises of mindful breathing offer us some practices of concentration that can help liberate us from the craving, anger, fear, and delusion that have perpetuated our suffering.

In the Buddhist tradition we speak of many practices of

concentration. One concentration that's widely practiced and very beneficial is the contemplation on impermanence. We know that all things are impermanent, yet in our daily lives we carry on as though things were permanent. The contemplation on impermanence can help us to be free from many afflictions such as anger and fear.

Suppose you're angry with your partner. He just said something that made you suffer deeply. You suffer so much that you have a desire to say something back in order to make him suffer. You believe that if you can say something to make him suffer, you will suffer less. We're intelligent enough to know this is childish behavior, but many of us still do it anyway. If you say something that makes him suffer, then he'll try to get relief by saying something back that makes you suffer. Both of you are practicing the escalation of anger.

Suppose instead you practice the concentration on impermanence.

Breathing in, I observe the
impermanent nature of all things.
Breathing out, I contemplate the
impermenent nature of all things.

You don't say anything; you just close your eyes and breathe in.

In the three or four seconds of breathing in, you visualize how your loved one will be three hundred years from now:

What will he be three hundred years from now?
What will I have become three hundred years from now?

The concentration on impermanence right away brings you the insight that he is impermanent, that you are impermanent, and that it's silly to make each other suffer like this in the present moment. The concentration on impermanence will bring the insight of impermanence, allowing you to touch in a very real way the nature of impermanence in him and in you at the same time. Breathing in, you practice the concentration on impermanence. Breathing out, you already have the insight of impermanence. When you open your eyes, you're so happy that he is still alive, the only thing you want to do is open your arms and hug him.

Breathing in, darling, I know that you are still alive.
Breathing out, I am so happy.

It isn't the idea or notion of impermanence but the insight of impermanence that can free you and save you. Intellectually all of us know that everything is impermanent. But in our daily lives we still behave as if things are permanent. Impermanence is not a negative note in the song of life. If there were no impermanence, life would be impossible. Without impermanence how could your little girl grow up and become a beautiful woman? Without impermanence how could you hope to transform your suffering? You can hope to transform your suffering because you know your suffering is impermanent. So impermanence is a positive note. We should say, "Long live impermanence!"

14. NON-CRAVING

The fourteenth exercise is contemplating non-craving.

Breathing in, I observe the disappearance of desire.
Breathing out, I observe the disappearance of desire.

Unless we practice mindfulness we don't realize that we already have enough conditions to be happy in the here and the now. That's what prevents us from being happy here and now. We try to run after the objects of our craving such as fame, wealth, and power. When we look around, we may see people who have plenty of these things but who continue to suffer very deeply. How much power do we need to be happy? The president is supposed to be the most powerful man in the United States, but I think he feels he doesn't have enough power. He wants to do so many things, but he lacks the power to make them happen. If you think that having power or lots of money is what you need in order to be happy, that's a wrong view. There are so many wealthy people who don't have enough understanding and love in them, and they suffer very deeply from loneliness.

When a fisherman wants to catch a fish, he throws a line into the river so the fish will see the bait and bite down on the hook hidden inside. If the fish hasn't seen the hook inside the bait, she will bite, get hooked, and die. We have to breathe in and look deeply into the object of our craving and see the many dangers hidden within it. Running after that particular object of your craving may destroy your body and your mind. We see many people destroying themselves by running after the objects of their craving. At the same time there are other people who see that true happiness is made of understanding and love. The more they cultivate understanding and love, the happier they become. That is how contemplating non-craving saves you and helps you to be liberated from your craving.

15. NIRVANA

The fifteenth exercise is the contemplation of nirvana.

Breathing in, I contemplate nirvana.
Breathing out, I contemplate nirvana.

Nirvana is our true nature of no birth and no death, no being and no nonbeing. Nirvana is insight; it's the freedom from all kinds of notions. It's possible to touch our nature of nirvana during this very life, right here and now. The Buddhist term "nirvana" is equivalent to the term "God" in Christianity, Judaism, or Islam. There is a Buddhist scripture called Enjoyment of What Is Beyond Space and Time, in which nirvana is talked about in very lovely, positive terms. There's a verse, "Deer take refuge in the forests, birds in the clouds of the sky. Those who practice the truth depend on nirvana to live in freedom."

Nirvana is available in the here and now. Many people in the Christian tradition use the beautiful phrase "resting in God." Allowing yourself to rest in God is like a wave resting in its essential nature, the water. Imagine a wave rising and falling on the surface of the ocean. Observing the wave, we can see it has a beginning and an ending; it comes up and it goes down. The notions of beginning, ending, going up, and going down may scare the wave and she may think, "Before rising up as this wave, I didn't exist, and soon I will become nothing again." It seems as if before the wave comes up it's not there, and after it goes down it no longer exists. How could a wave be a happy wave if she's caught in these notions of birth and death, beginning and ending, going up and going down? But there's a way out, an opportunity for her to be saved. When she bends down and examines herself, she discovers that she is water. She's a wave, but she's also water. As a wave she may be described in terms of being and nonbeing, coming and going. But water cannot be described in these terms. The moment the wave realizes she's water, she's free—free from such notions as birth and death, coming up and going down. The wave is water right in the here and the now.

Just as the wave doesn't need to go looking for water, we don't need to go around seeking nirvana or God. We can enjoy nirvana right away. Just as the wave can rest in water, we can rest in God in the here and the now. With mindfulness and concentration we are able to touch our true nature of no birth and no death.

We know that a cloud can never die; it can only become snow, rain, or ice. A cloud can never become nothing. The true nature of no birth and no death is there in everything, including ourselves. The cloud can look at the rain and smile, and be free from fear. To be the cloud floating in the sky is a wonderful thing, and to become the rain falling down on the Earth and nourishing everything is also a wonderful thing. To become a river, to become a cup of tea for people to drink is also wonderful. To become water vapor and become a cloud again is also something wonderful. Our true nature is the nature of no birth and no death. We know that this insight corresponds with what science has found, that "nothing is born, nothing dies; everything is in transformation." That is the first law of thermodynamics.

16. LETTING GO

The last exercise of mindful breathing is the practice of releasing notions, letting go. Notions of birth and death, being and nonbeing are the foundation of our fear and anxiety. Letting go of these notions makes you free, and you can touch your true nature: you can be in touch with God.

To understand the teachings of teachers like the Buddha or Jesus, you have to remove your dualistic way of thinking. Many of us misunderstand the teachings of the Buddha and of Jesus. If we're caught in dualistic thinking, when we observe a father and son, we see them as two completely different people. But when we look deeply into the person of the son, we see the father in each cell of the son. Even if you get angry with your father, even if you don't want to have anything to do with him ever again, you can't remove your father from you. Your father is present in every cell of your body.

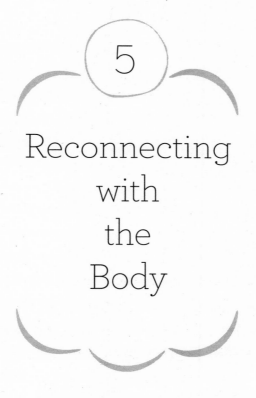

5

Reconnecting
with
the
Body

Most of us walk around with pains and tension in our bodies. We may think of this as normal or natural or just part of aging. But it's possible to move freely without tension if we can heal the division of body and mind. Even if we have some kind of ailment that causes us physical discomfort, we don't need to have tension around this pain, compounding it. We don't need to cause more suffering.

How can we bring relief and healing to our bodies? We may think only a medical doctor can look into our body to know what's happening and heal us. We put all our faith in somebody else. It's similar to the relationship some of us have to religion. We put our belief wholly into a deity who we believe can save us. But in reality, the basis for healing is to be in touch with ourselves, with our own bodies.

Breathing in, I'm aware that I have a body.
Breathing out, I recognize that my body is there.

In that in-breath and out-breath we find a way to be in touch with our body.

Sickness Comes from the Disconnection of Body and Mind

Can you calculate in how many moments out of twenty-four hours your body and mind are in harmony? Your mind very seldom stays with your body. It has the tendency to wander off.

How much time does each of us spend in front of the computer? There are people who spend more than twelve hours on the computer every day. In that time, they completely forget they have a body. There are other things like the phone and the television that make us forget our bodies. We have many distractions that take our minds away from being in touch with our bodies. We actually forget we have a body! How can we not get sick? It's inevitable.

If we can't be in touch with our bodies, we can't really be in touch with our minds. Body and mind are two sides of a coin; we can't separate them. When the mind is wandering around outside, we don't really know what's happening within the mind or the body. We don't know how to embrace our worry, sadness, and anger, so we cover up our alienation with consumption: reading magazines, listening to music, watching videos, drinking wine, taking drugs, or eating when we're not hungry. We eat in order to forget. When we eat, we think we can forget our suffering, our sadness, our worry, and we eat too much. Humans are sick today because they're out of touch with their bodies and they can't be in touch with their minds. How then is it possible to be in touch with the source of health, Mother Earth? If you can be in touch with your body, you have an opportunity to be in touch with Mother Earth, your source.

Embracing Our Suffering

Everyone has the seed of suffering inside. Sometimes it slumbers in the depths of our consciousness and sometimes it manifests as a very noticeable energy. When suffering manifests, it's difficult to feel joy or happiness. The practice of conscious breathing and mindful walking or mindful sitting, can help us handle the suffering inside. Our suffering is not only our own suffering. It carries within it the suffering of our father, our mother, and the many ancestors who have transmitted it to us.

Our suffering also reflects the suffering of our people, our country, our society, and our world. When we understand the nature and the roots of our suffering, then compassion and love can arise. We go home to ourselves and get in touch with the suffering inside and hold it tenderly. This is our practice. We can do the same with our fear. Practicing conscious breathing, we generate the energy of mindfulness and concentration. These are the energies with which we can recognize and embrace our suffering. If we don't have the energy of mindfulness, the suffering may overwhelm us. But if we breathe in and out and allow our body to be relaxed, we can generate the energy of mindfulness and concentration, and with that energy we can embrace and take care of our suffering. You just accept your suffering and hold it tenderly.

My dear suffering, I know you are there in me.
I am here to take care of you.

Suffering and Happiness Inter-Are

There are people who wish to find a place where there is no suffering, like heaven, the Pure Land of the Buddha, or the kingdom of God. We may think that "up there" there is no suffering—there is only happiness. But when we look deeply we see that suffering and happiness inter-are, just as the mud and the lotus interpenetrate each other. A lotus can only grow in mud. If there were no mud, there would be no lotus flower. There's a very close connection between suffering and happiness, just as there is between mud and lotus. Real happiness is possible when we have the right view of suffering and happiness. It's the same as front and back, right and left. The right cannot exist without the left; the left cannot exist without the right. Happiness cannot exist without suffering.

Happiness is made of non-happiness elements, just as the flower is made of non-flower elements. When you look at the flower, you see non-flower elements like sunlight, rain, earth—all the elements that have come together to help the flower to manifest. If we were to remove any of those non-flower elements there would no longer be a flower. Happiness is a kind of flower. If you look deeply into happiness, you see non-happiness elements, including suffering. Suffering plays a very important role in happiness. When we look into a lotus flower, we see the mud in it. This view of happiness is the right view. There are even Buddhist scholars and practitioners who don't realize that the first teaching that the Buddha gave regarding suffering was also about happiness.

When we live mindfully, we try to live in such a way that we can continue to generate the energies of mindfulness, concentration, and insight. These are the energies that bring us happiness and the clarity that we call "Right View." When we have Right View, we're able to practice Right Thinking. Right Thinking is based on Right View; it's thinking that's characterized by nondiscrimination and nonduality.

There's a very deep connection between suffering and happiness. We've seen how a flower is made only of non-flower elements—it is made of the soil, the sun, the rain. We've seen that a lotus flower needs to be rooted in the mud. In the same way, happiness cannot be there in the absence of suffering. If we have the idea that there's a place where suffering doesn't exist, where there's only happiness, that isn't correct. It's not Right Thinking because it's not based on Right View. According to Right View, there can be no happiness without suffering. Our thinking can make us suffer. But our thinking can also make us free. We need Right Thinking to help us stop our suffering, so we can begin to have more happiness.

If there's a group of people living in the same environment, some may be happy and others unhappy. There are those among us who have the ability to appreciate the presence of the sun, who can get in touch with the trees, the fog, and all the wonders of life that are around us and inside us. But there are some people who don't have the ability to get in touch with these wonderful things. They only see suffering. The conditions of their lives are exactly the same as those of the people who are happy, so why are some people happy and others not happy? The answer is that the one who is happy has Right View. The other is suffering because he doesn't have Right View, so his thinking is not Right Thinking. Suffering is relative. Something that causes one person to suffer may not cause another person to suffer.

Full Presence in the Body

With the practice of mindful breathing and mindful walking, we bring our mind back to our body. When the body and mind are together, we can establish ourselves in the here and the now and we can get in touch with life and all its wonders. So we may like to say to ourselves, "Breathing in, I am aware that my body is here." Breathing in, coming back to the body, and getting in touch with the body—that is already mindfulness: mindfulness that my body is here and that it is a wonder.

Our feelings, emotions, and perceptions often feel like they're overwhelming our bodies and minds. Mindfulness helps us to get in touch with all these things that are going on. Body, feelings, and perceptions are objects of our mindfulness. There are many other beautiful things inside us and around us that we can also make the objects of our mindfulness. Every morning when we wake up, we can breathe in and get in touch with the miracle that is life. There are things that are wonderful, that can nourish and heal us. Mindfulness puts us in touch with those things for our own healing and happiness. That is the first function of mindfulness: joy. Mindfulness brings us joy and happiness.

Practice: Body Scan

There is an exercise for releasing the tension in the body as a whole and releasing the tension in each part. We can begin by paying attention to the whole body and then different parts of the body. Begin with the head, or the hair on the head, and finish with the toes.

Breathing in, I am aware of my brain.
Breathing out, I smile to my brain.

Use the conscious mind to recognize that a certain part of the body is there. In this way, we can recognize and embrace it with the energy of mindfulness, and allow that part of the body to relax and release the tension. Then you come down to the eyes.

Breathing in, I'm aware of my eyes.
Breathing out, I smile to my eyes.

Allow your eyes to release the tension that is in and around the eyes. A light smile can help you to relax. You can go on to send that smile to different parts of your body.

In your face there are dozens of muscles, and when you get angry or fearful there's a lot of tension in all these muscles. If you breathe in and are aware of them, and breathe out and smile to them, you can help them to release the tension. Your face can be completely relaxed after just one in-breath and out-breath. Your smile can bring about a miracle.

Breathing in, I smile.
Breathing out, I allow all the muscles in my face to relax.

Then you come to your shoulders, and then your heart. Then to your left arm, and your right arm, always recognizing them with the energy of mindfulness and smiling to them and helping them to release the tension. It's like scanning the body—not with an x-ray, but with the ray of your mindfulness. You take the time, perhaps ten or fifteen minutes, to scan your body with the energy of mindfulness. Smiling to every part of your body, you help that part of the body to relax and release tension.

When we come to a part of the body that is ailing, we can stay there longer. We should spend more time recognizing and embracing that part of our body with the energy of mindfulness. Embrace it, smile to it, and help it to release the tension. Practicing this exercise will help you heal. If you have to use some drugs for a physical ailment, please don't rely on them alone. When you know how to help release the tension in that part of the body, the healing happens much more quickly. When there's a physical pain, your mindfulness will tell you that it's only a physical pain, and with that kind of awareness you won't exaggerate anything or worsen the pain because of fear and tension.

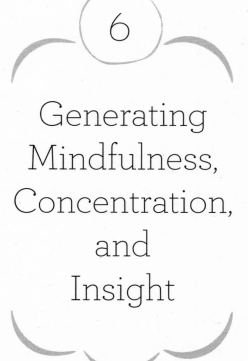

6

Generating
Mindfulness,
Concentration,
and
Insight

True life is possible only with mindfulness and concentration. If you're in a state of dispersion, you are lost. The thinking we do in this kind of state is very seldom beneficial. Thinking can be productive and good. But most of our thinking is not productive. Our thoughts pull us away from the here and the now. It's only in the here and the now that we can encounter real life, that we can be in touch with our body and the other wonders of life available in the here and the now. So we think, and we get lost in our thinking, and we're not there for life. It's very important to learn how to stop all that thinking. It doesn't mean that thinking is inherently bad, because in fact, thinking can be good. But so much of our thinking causes sorrow, fear, or anger to arise. We need to learn to stop thinking, in order to begin to feel—feel the presence of our body, feel the presence of the wonders of life that are available in the here and the now. If you can feel their presence, you can get the nourishment and healing that you need—from the sunshine, the fresh air, the beautiful trees, your lungs, your in-breath and out-breath.

During the time you breathe in, you become aware once again that you have a body. There's a kind of happy reunion between mind and body. It may take only a few seconds for you to become anchored back home in the here and the now so that you can truly live your life. We have to be in the here and the now in order to be alive. The past is no longer with us and the future is not yet here; only in the present moment are the wonders of life available. The secret of meditation is to bring the mind home to the body and be in the here and the now. It's very simple. Stopping the thinking will help tremendously.

Mindfulness, Concentration, and Insight

When you're practicing mindfulness of your body, your body becomes the only object of your mindfulness.

Breathing in, I know my body is there.
Breathing out, I know my body is there,

When mindfulness is strong and focused like that, concentration is born. The object of your concentration is also your body. When mindfulness and concentration are powerful enough, you can make a breakthrough into reality, and you get insight, realization, and you discover things. Mindfulness, or *smrti* in Sanskrit, is the first energy. Mindfulness brings about concentration, *samadhi*, the second energy, and together mindfulness and concentration bring insight, *prajña*.

To meditate means to generate these three kinds of energies. You don't have to ask for them to come to you from outside. Everyone has the seeds of mindfulness, concentration, and insight within himself or herself. With the practice of mindful breathing, mindful walking, mindful sitting, we help these seeds to manifest as energies. These are the three kinds of energy that make an enlightened being. They make you awake, bring your body and mind fully together, and put you in touch with all the wonders of life. You stop running and trying to look for happiness somewhere else. You see that happiness is possible in the here and the now.

Joy and happiness are possible right away when mindfulness and concentration are strong enough. You rediscover that your body is there; that all the wonders of life are there; that so many conditions of happiness are already available. This is already insight. This insight can help you to be free from your worries, your fear, your longing and searching. That kind of insight helps you to recognize there are more than enough conditions for you to be happy right here and right now. Insight brings freedom, joy, and happiness.

When you're fully aware of what is there, and you can

maintain that awareness and keep concentration alive, then insight arises. When you're mindful of the presence of a flower, and you sustain that awareness, that is concentration. Concentration is born from mindfulness; the energy of mindfulness is the bearer of concentration. If you practice mindfulness deeply, concentration is there, and with that concentration you're able to look deeply into what is going on and you will make a breakthrough into reality.

Holiness Is Mindfulness, Concentration, and Insight

These three energies can be generated by practicing mindfulness of breathing, walking, sitting, and all your other daily activities. When you are inhabited by these three wholesome energies, there is holiness in you.

We speak of holiness, but oftentimes we don't know exactly what it is. To me it's very clear that holiness is made of mindfulness, concentration, and insight. When you're inhabited by these three energies, you are a buddha, an enlightened person. In Christianity we speak of the Holy Spirit. The Holy Spirit can be interpreted as the quality of presence that is there when we have mindfulness, concentration, and insight. Wherever these three energies are, life is there, healing is there, nourishment and happiness are there. So it's possible to generate the energy of holiness. When these energies of holiness are in you, you don't suffer anymore; you're free. I can call you "Your Holiness." Everyone can be holy if they know how to generate the energy of mindfulness, concentration, and insight. It's not too difficult.

When I pour tea, I like to pour the tea mindfully. When I pour the tea mindfully, my mind isn't in the past, in the future, or with my projects. My mind is focused on pouring the tea. I'm fully concentrated on the act of pouring tea. Pouring tea becomes the only object of my mindfulness and concentration. That is a pleasure and it also can bring many insights. I can see that in the tea there is a cloud. Yesterday it was a cloud. But today it is my tea. Insight is not something very far away. With mindfulness and concentration you can begin to get the insight that can liberate you and bring you happiness.

There is mindfulness of breathing, mindfulness of pouring tea, mindfulness of drinking tea, mindfulness of walking, mindfulness of breathing, mindfulness of brushing teeth, and so on. When you breathe mindfully, you focus your attention only on one thing, your in- or out-breath that is happening. You are concentrated on your breath. When you are really concentrated on your breath, insight can come right away. You may get the insight that you are fully alive, and to be fully alive like that is a miracle.

Insight Is Not
Something Far Away

Insight is enlightenment, awakening. You're enlightened about the fact that you are alive. You wake up once again to the miraculous reality that you are there, still alive. There are many insights that can happen while you breathe in mindfully. You breathe in and you realize that your legs are still strong enough for you to walk, jump, and run. There are those of us who can no longer walk. When I practice walking, I'm very happy and grateful that I can still walk. Many of my friends from my generation can't walk anymore. But I'm still capable of using my feet and walking with my friends. Just walking can bring a lot of happiness.

Thanks to mindfulness, concentration, and insight, every step can generate the energy of joy and happiness. That is meditation. Bringing your mind home to your body, establishing yourself in the present moment and touching the wonders of life makes joy, happiness, and freedom possible in the here and the now. Everyone can do it.

Everyone can pour his tea mindfully. Everyone can drink her tea mindfully. Instead of allowing ourselves to think of the past or the future, we just focus our mindfulness on drinking tea. We are fully present in the here and the now. The only thing we touch is the tea. If I'm mindful of my body and am established in the here and the now, I become so much more real. When I'm real, life is also real. The tea I'm holding in my hands is real. It's because I'm real that the tea becomes real. The encounter between the tea and me is real; that's real life. If you're possessed by fear, anger, or ruminative thinking, you're not truly there and your tea is not truly there. It's not true life.

Generating the Energy of Mindfulness Is the Basic Practice

The energy of mindfulness makes things real and alive. The practices of mindful walking, mindful sitting, and mindful breathing help generate the energy of mindfulness and are the basic practice. You can take a shower in mindfulness and enjoy the entire time of taking a shower. When you prepare your breakfast, if you allow mindfulness to be there in every moment, you can enjoy making breakfast and it can be a time of genuine happiness. Every moment of making breakfast can be a delight. When you wash the dishes you can wash the same way— breathing in, feeling your aliveness, standing at the sink and recognizing that the water is flowing. Water has come from far away into your kitchen. Getting in touch with water and washing each plate and bowl in mindfulness can be a joy. You don't need to hurry to finish washing dishes. You can enjoy washing your dishes. Washing dishes in this way is just as profound and holy as doing sitting meditation or walking meditation.

When you go to the toilet, you may choose to urinate in mindfulness. You take the time and enjoy urinating. Why hurry? This time is given to us to live. It can be a very pleasant moment. Happiness and freedom are possible during the time you urinate. You don't want to do it in a hurry so that you can go off and do other things. This is why in meditation centers we put a flowerpot in the toilet room, to remind us that this is also a meditation hall. Enjoy the time when you take your shower. Enjoy the time when you prepare your breakfast. Enjoy the time when you urinate or defecate. It can be very pleasant.

When you brush your teeth, brush in a way that makes freedom and joy possible. You have two or three minutes of tooth brushing. Make them into a happy moment of life. If you can be happy during the time of brushing your teeth, then buttoning up your jacket can also be a joy. Every moment of your daily life can be a happy moment if you know how to allow mindfulness and concentration to be present. With mindfulness and concentration, we can enjoy every moment that is given us to live. That is the art of living.

Freedom from the Past and Future

We need freedom. But freedom from what? We need freedom from our sorrow and regret concerning the past. The past may have become a prison we can't escape from. Mindfulness helps us get out of the prison of the past and to be here now with the present moment

The future can also be a prison. Many of us are afraid, uncertain, and anxious about the future. The future has become a prison to us. We have to get out of that prison. Breathing in, bringing the mind home to the body and coming back to the present moment is already liberation. The three kinds of energies of mindfulness, concentration, and insight are agents of liberation; they can help us to be free. True happiness is not possible without freedom.

We have to learn the habit of being free. When we sit, we sit as a free person—light, happy, enjoying our body and the time of sitting. When we walk, we walk like a free person. We don't allow the past, the future, our projects, or our fear to get hold of us. We are free. We relish every step. Every step is freedom. Every step is nourishment. Every step is healing. Every step is joy. We can borrow from the collective energy of the group that is walking mindfully with us. We flow like a river. Walking like that is a celebration of life. Every step is a celebration. We arrive in the here and the now. We arrive in the kingdom of God, in the Pure

Land of the Buddha with every step.

You Are a Bell of Mindfulness

When I see you established in the present moment, walking with ease, mindfully and happily, I know that you are in the kingdom of God, in the Pure Land of the Buddha, and I am inspired to walk like you. I breathe in and I'm aware of my in-breath. I make a step and I'm aware that I'm alive. I touch the beautiful bodhisattva, the great Earth, and I also arrive in the Pure Land of the Buddha, the kingdom of God.

So your practice is very helpful. You just walk mindfully and breathe mindfully, and all of us will benefit from your practice. You're a bell of mindfulness. You remind us to come home to the here and the now and become alive again. You may think you're not doing anything for us, but that's not true. You're walking mindfully, enjoying every step, and you're generating the energy of joy and happiness in yourself. You are helping us. We need people like you, happy people, free people, joyful people. When we see you walking like that, we want to do like you.

Collective Energy of Practice

When we practice together as a group we generate a collective energy of mindfulness and peace that can help heal and nourish us and our children. Practicing together, we have the opportunity to produce the powerful, collective energy of mindfulness, compassion, concentration, insight, and joy that can help change the world. We don't need more money, fame, or wealth in order to be happy. Just generating these three kinds of energies, we can create freedom and happiness for ourselves and for many people around us. We have a chance to be together. Walking from one place to another, why don't we enjoy every step? We are here for that. Enjoy every step. Give yourself pleasure, joy, and freedom with every step.

Stop Running

We have a habit of running. We've been running for a long time. Now, we have to recognize that habit, stop running, and learn to live our life properly and deeply. We can be supported by our brothers and sisters in the practice. This is why we come together. After one week it may become our new habit to walk happily, breathe happily, sit happily, eat happily, brush our teeth happily. To learn to live mindfully and to be happy in every moment, to learn in every moment is a good habit to develop. We don't need to wait until tomorrow or some time in the future to be happy. What are we waiting for to be happy? Why are we waiting to start celebrating? We can celebrate now. Every step is to celebrate life, thanks to mindfulness, concentration, and insight.

Generating Joy

"Breathing in, I bring in a pleasant feeling, a feeling of joy." This is not mere imagination or wishful thinking. It's possible to generate these feelings with mindfulness. Breathing in mindfully, you may get the insight that so many conditions of happiness are available right this minute. Your feet are strong, your eyes are still in good condition, your ears can hear all kinds of sounds, and you can enjoy walking. Walking meditation becomes a pleasure, a delight. When you touch the conditions of happiness with mindfulness, joy is born naturally—the joy of being alive, the joy of having opportunities to practice, to heal, to nourish, to release tension, and the joy of practicing with others. We should be able to bring in a feeling of joy anytime we want, at any time of the day, just by using mindfulness and recognizing that we are luckier than many other people. There are people who are caught in situations of war, political oppression, and imprisonment. There are people suffering from grave social injustice. But right now, we are here in an environment that has enough freedom. We have fresh air, we have a place to walk, a place to sit, we have something to eat, we don't have to walk ten miles to fetch water to drink. There are many conditions of happiness available. We overlook them. We take them for granted. We don't treasure them. Mindfulness helps us to recognize them and cherish them. With that kind of attention, that kind of mindfulness, we can produce joy; and with that mindfulness and joy, we can help others to wake up and realize that they are lucky also. "Darling, don't you see that we are very lucky?" Producing a feeling of joy is possible at any moment.

Producing Happiness

In my tradition, we see there's a little bit of difference between joy and happiness. In the experience of joy, there is some excitement involved. But in tasting happiness, you feel more calm, more contented. If you're very thirsty and there's nothing for you to drink, you suffer. Then if suddenly you hear someone say, "Somebody is getting you a bottle of water," just hearing that, you have joy in the anticipation, even though you're not drinking the water yet. But once you're actually drinking the water, you experience happiness.

With practice, we can always bring in a feeling of joy or happiness at any time. One aspect of meditation is developing the capacity to generate the energy of joy and happiness for our nourishment. We don't need more money, power, or fame to be happier with life. There are many people who have plenty of these things but are not truly happy. When we have freedom, insight, mindfulness, concentration, we can be happy right here and right now. Just sitting, just breathing, just taking a shower, just brushing our teeth, just walking—doing these things with mindful appreciation can be a lot of happiness already. Part of practicing well is knowing how to produce joy and happiness and keep them alive as long as we wish.

Practicing with Others

It's easier when we can practice with friends on the path. We can create a collective body when we practice full-body meditation together. When we hear the sound of the meditation bell, for example, we know everyone is breathing, going back to themselves, and creating the energy of mindfulness. The collective energy of mindfulness is very powerful, very effective, and transformative. We can benefit from that energy and use it to help embrace our pain and our suffering. In Vietnam there's a saying, "When you eat rice, you need to have soup." When you practice, you have to have friends.

Practice: Taking Refuge

Taking refuge is the recognition and the determination to go in the direction of what is beatufiul, good, and true. Taking refuge is also to be in touch with our capacity to love, understand, and see clearly.

When we find ourselves in dangerous or difficult situations, or when we feel like we are losing ourselves, we can practice taking refuge. Instead of panicking or giving ourselves up to despair, we can put our trust in the power of self-healing, self-understanding, and loving within us. We call this the island within ourselves in which we can take refuge. It is an island of peace, confidence, solidity, love, and freedom. Be an island within yourself. You don't have to look for it elsewhere.

We want to feel safe and protected. We want to feel calm. So when a situation seems to be turbulent, overwhelming, full of suffering, we have to practice taking refuge in the Buddha, the Buddha in ourselves. Each of us has the seed of Buddhahood, the capacity for being calm, understanding, compassionate, and for taking refuge in the island of safety within us so we can maintain our humanness, our peace, our hope. Practicing like this, we become an island of peace and compassion, and we may inspire others to do the same.

We are like a boat crossing the ocean. If the boat encounters a storm and everyone panics, the boat will turn over. If there is one person in the boat who can remain calm, that person can inspire other people to be calm. Then there will be hope for the whole boatload. Who is that person who can stay calm in the situation of distress? Each of us is that person. We count on each other.

Use this gatha to return to yourself, wherever you are:

Breathing in, I go back to the island within myself.
There are beautiful trees within the island.
There are cool streams of water,
there are birds, sunshine, and fresh air.
Breathing out, I feel safe.

7

Steady in
the Storm

If you have an unpleasant feeling, a feeling of sadness, fear, worry, or despair, you may think you don't have the capacity to return home to be in touch with that emotion, to manage and embrace it. You want to run away from it—and you have many ways to run away, like magazines, books, music, food, the Internet, or busily strategizing—so you won't be in touch with your body and mind. Mind and body are alienated from each other, and this makes us sick.

When some catastrophe happens, when you have a painful feeling in your body, when something isn't going well, when you have a strong emotion, mindfulness will help you to be aware of it, and you will be able to do something to soothe and calm that pain. Mindfulness puts you in touch with the positive things, and it can also help you be present and skillful with things that are unpleasant.

Handling Anger

You may have anger. Anger can ravage your mind and body. But if you can breathe mindfully, come back to the present moment, and get in touch with your body and with your feelings and embrace them, there is already some relief. "Breathing in, I know that anger is in me. Breathing out, I embrace my anger." There's already a difference. If we don't practice mindfulness and embracing, then there's just the anger, that one energy, in us. Left to its own devices, that energy can push us to say and do things that will cause damage.

So when the anger comes up, you practice. You practice mindful breathing, and you generate the energy of mindfulness.

Breathing in, I know that anger is there in me.
Breathing out, I embrace the anger in me.

There's the energy of anger, but there's also the energy of mindfulness being produced, which is recognizing and embracing the anger.

The energy of mindfulness embraces and calms the anger: "My little anger, I am here for you; I'm going to take good care of you." Mindfulness will help you to handle the suffering. The essential thing is to light up your mindfulness and to have that second energy that can recognize the suffering or the anger and patiently and tenderly embrace that pain. Then two energies will be operating, the suffering energy and the mindfulness that recognizes and embraces that suffering. If you practice in this way you will obtain relief very quickly. That is the second function of mindfulness. First of all, with mindfulness we can nourish and heal ourselves with positive things. Secondly, with mindfulness we can embrace and relieve our suffering.

Restlessness

The peace, calm, and harmony you produce in your breathing will penetrate into your body and your mind. Even if you're feeling restless, the energy of mindful breathing will encounter your energy of restlessness, and in no time at all you'll see a change as the energy of restlessness steadily ebbs away and transforms. Someone who has the habit of doing this practice can, in just one or two breaths, completely transform restlessness and feel peaceful. Whatever you learn, whatever insight you gain from practice should be applied right away in your daily life. In that way you develop your confidence and find that you have faith in your practice.

When the mind is restless or angry, allow it to be embraced with the energy of mindfulness. Don't try to change your restlessness. Don't try to push it away or suppress it. Just allow it to be. Continue to breathe and to generate the energy of mindfulness. Recognize the feeling of restlessness or anger and embrace it tenderly. As the two kinds of energy—the energy of restlessness and the energy of mindfulness—encounter each other, there will be a change, and transformation will take place. In the energy of mindfulness there is peace and concentration. Even just being aware that you're restless or angry will already bring some change. In the beginning it may be 5 or 10 percent. As you continue to follow your breathing, there will be a complete change, and loving kindness, the opposite of anger, will arise.

Taking Refuge in Consumption

If we don't have a way of connecting body and mind, we may try to disassociate even further, to numb our suffering. We try to run away from our suffering through consumption, perhaps by surfing the web, listening to music, eating, or striking up a conversation.

When you're sad, angry, or lonely, and you don't know how to take care of your sadness, your loneliness, your anger, you may go open the refrigerator and take out something to eat even though you're not hungry and you don't need it. You eat to forget your suffering, because you don't know how to handle it. We may seek to cover up our suffering by reading the newspaper, magazines, or books, watching television, and so on. We're running away from our suffering. That is what we tend to do. We don't have the courage to come back home to ourselves and take care of our suffering.

In the practice of mindfulness we do the opposite. We

practice mindful walking; we practice mindful breathing to generate the energy of mindfulness and concentration. With that kind of energy we go home to our fear, and we say, "My dear suffering, my dear despair and anger, I know you are there. I am home; I'm here to take care of you."

We can learn how to handle a painful feeling, a painful emotion whenever it begins to manifest. We have to come home and tell the pain in us,

> Breathing in, I know you are there, my pain.
> Breathing out, I will take good care of you.

You're not running away. You're coming back home to take care of your pain. If you need to, you can ask a few brothers and sisters to support you by producing the collective energy of mindfulness to help you recognize and embrace your pain. Using the energy of mindfulness, we can acknowledge and be there for the pain, the sorrow, the fear inside us.

When suffering arises, we need to know how to deal with it. We shouldn't let it overwhelm us. We can use mindfulness. When a painful feeling arises in us, running away or suppressing it will only make it persist. We need to be present and say, "I am here for you." We need to practice mindful breathing, mindful steps to generate the energy of mindfulness.

Breathing in, I recognize my painful feeling.
Breathing out, I recognize my painful feeling.

With that energy we acknowledge our suffering, our pain, and we embrace it and calm it down.

Breathing in, I embrace my painful feeling.
Breathing out, I calm my painful feeling.

We come back to our body and we calm down the tension and pain in our body. When we're able to calm our body, then we can calm our feelings and our emotions.

Practice: Belly Breathing

When we have a strong emotion, we know we don't need to be afraid, because we have ways to take care of a strong emotion. We need some insight; we need some practice. When the strong emotion arises, we say to it, "You are only an emotion."

An emotion is something that comes, stays for some time, and eventually goes away. There are many young people who don't know how to handle a strong emotion. They believe that the only way to end the emotion and the suffering is to kill themselves. That's why so many young people commit suicide in our time. It's important for them to learn that an emotion is just one emotion, and that it's very tiny compared with the totality of our person.

Our person is made of body, feelings, perceptions, mental formations, and consciousness. The territory is vast. You are not only an emotion you're having. You are much more than one emotion. That is the insight you should have when the emotion comes up. "Hello, my emotion. I know you are there. I will take care of you." You practice mindfully breathing deep into your abdomen, and you know that you can handle that storm in you.

Sit down in the lotus position, or any seated position in which you're comfortable; or you can lie down. Put your hand on your stomach, breathe in very deeply, breathe out very deeply, and become aware of the rising and falling of your abdomen. "Breathing in, my abdomen is rising. Breathing out, my abdomen is falling." Completely concentrate on the rising and falling of your abdomen. Stop all thinking. The more you think about your emotion, the stronger it will become.

When taking care of a strong emotion, don't allow yourself to dwell at the level of your head, of your thinking. Bring your awareness down to your abdomen, just below the navel. Become aware only of the rising and falling of your abdomen. Stick to this, and you will be safe. It's like a tree standing in a storm. When you look at the top of the tree, you see that the upper branches and leaves are swaying violently back and forth in the wind. You may have the impression that the tree is going to be broken or blown away. But when you direct your attention to the trunk of the tree, you see that part of the tree is not swaying, you see that the tree is firmly and deeply rooted, and you have a different feeling. You know the tree is going to withstand the storm. When there's an emotional storm going on inside you, don't get stuck up there in your head where thoughts are racing through. Stop the thinking. Go down and embrace the trunk of your body, down at the level of the abdomen. Focus your attention 100 percent on the rise and fall of your abdomen, and you'll be safe. As long as you maintain mindful breathing and keep your full attention only on the rising and falling of your abdomen, you are safe. You may need to do this for twenty minutes or so. But if you stay with it, the insight will come that you are much more than one emotion.

With this practice you can survive a powerful emotion very easily. But don't wait until that emotion comes to begin doing the practice. You'll naturally forget. You have to begin training in it right now. If every day you practice mindful abdominal breathing for five or ten minutes, you'll naturally remember to practice when the emotion comes, and you'll survive the emotion very easily. And each time that happens, you'll have more and more confidence that the next time a strong emotion comes along, you will not be afraid anymore, because you know how to handle it.

8

Taking
Care of
Body
and
Mind

Our practice is being present, being fully present right here and right now. We're present to be in touch with the miracles of life, to be nourished, to heal, and to have transformation. We're present so we're able to recognize suffering and know how to embrace it and transform it into nourishing elements. How can we be fully present if we don't take care of ourselves?

Taking Care of Our Territory

To work in the garden you need to be there in the garden. Being present in the garden, you're able to take care of the different flowers, trees, and vegetables, and such a garden can nourish you and make your life more beautiful. If anything's become wilted, broken, or rotten, we can help it transform and become compost that can nourish the trees and flowers. The gardener needs to take care of the garden. What is our garden? Our garden is our body, our feelings, our perceptions, our other mental formations, and our consciousness.

We need to be present for ourselves. Imagine there's a country that doesn't have a government, a king, a queen, or a president. There is nobody around to take care of the country. The country needs to have a form of government. It's the same with ourselves. We need to be present in our territory, to take care of our territory, because our territory is very large. We need to be the king or queen and govern our territory. We need to know what is precious and beautiful so we can protect it. We need to know what things aren't so beautiful in order to fix or transform them. We need to be a good queen or king and not run away from our country. There are people who don't want to be king, who just want to run away from that job, because they think that being king is so tiring!

We run away by watching television, going online, listening to music, or going to parties. We don't want to return to our homeland. We are kings or queens who don't take any responsibility. We need to become aware of our responsibility, to recognize that we need to be the sovereign, return to our territory, and take care of it.

We can learn the best ways to take care of our territory. Practicing mindfulness means we know how to do it. The Sutra on the Full Awareness of Breathing shows us all the essential methods with the sixteen exercises of mindful breathing.

Coming Back to the Body and Taking Care

First of all we come back to our breathing and practice the first exercise.

Breathing in, I know I'm breathing in.
Breathing out, I know I'm breathing out.

The breath is the royal road that returns us to our body. We come back to our body in order to take care of it, to decrease the stress and pain. We can learn methods for doing this, like total relaxation and following our breathing to calm our body and our feelings. Those are the first things we need to do. One in-breath can help calm down our whole body and help release the pain and tension we're holding there. During that time our mind already returns to our body.

The second exercise is to develop concentration.

Breathing in, I follow my in-breath.
Breathing out, I follow my out-breath.

Keeping mindfulness alive while following your in-breath and out-breath all the way through is already concentration, and it makes your presence solid.

Once we've returned to our body and we're truly present, we can take care of the other parts of our territory like our feelings, our emotions, and other mental formations. We breathe in and out mindfully and we recognize our entire body.

Breathing in, I'm aware of my whole body.
Breathing out, I'm aware of my whole body.

We bring our full awareness and presence to our body as a whole. That's the third exercise of mindful breathing. The fourth exercise is,

Breathing in, I release the tension in my body.
Breathing out, I release the tension in my body.

This is a very concrete practice. When you walk mindfully, take each step in that way, with ease. Calming the body and calming the mind will bring us peace. We only need to hold solidly to the method of mindful breathing, of mindful walking, and that is something we can do. We return to our body to recognize and become aware of our body, and we release tension and calm down our body.

Creating Happiness

It's possible to create joy and happiness right now. Using your breathing, your steps, your mindfulness, you produce that happiness. You can also help create happiness for the person beside you.

The method is very simple. Once we have become present, we're able to see that in our body and all around us there are so many conditions of happiness. This recognition is a fruit of practicing mindfulness and making ourselves present; we're able to see the conditions of happiness that are right there in front of us. Our eyes are bright, we can hear the birds sing, our body is still mobile and alive; it's not stiff like the body of a person who has died. When I'm practicing the Mindful Movements—the series of ten exercises that we do daily in Plum Village—I say, "Oh! I'm still alive. I'm raising my arms to the sky. I feel very happy."

This isn't something morbid or scary. We just become aware. "Ah, I have still have hands, and I'm not stiff as a board. I'm not about to be cremated." When we're aware of the conditions of happiness in that way, knowing that our legs and feet are strong, that our ears can still hear, then we see that the conditions of happiness are so plentiful. We just need to be truly present in the moment to enjoy them. That's one method of creating happiness.

Another method of creating happiness is comparing our current situation with tougher situations that we could be having now but, fortunately, we aren't. In each person's life there are times of difficulty and challenge. It might be an accident, a serious illness, or the passing away of a loved one. Sometimes we suffered as children and it was very difficult for us to find happiness. Each of us still has inside of us the impressions left by those experiences. But if right now we would bring up those images and compare them with our situation in the present moment, we can see very clearly how happiness can arise right away. We tend to take for granted the many causes for happiness that we have. We're unaware; we can't see how precious the conditions of happiness are that are available to us right now, that may not always have been there (or may not be there forever in the future). So the second method of creating happiness is bringing up the suffering that we've had in the past and comparing it with the conditions of happiness we have right now. It makes that happiness shine; you can see it more clearly. This is an art. It's very different from bringing up past suffering and being drowned in it.

There are people who've fought in the wars in Afghanistan or Iraq. Many of those who didn't die in the battlefield, who make it out of there alive, don't have the capacity to enjoy their good fortune to have survived, to live in the present moment once they return home. They keep returning to the past, getting themselves wrapped up in the memories of the suffering, the pain, and the difficulties that they encountered in the war, and they can't let go. In the present moment there are many things to treasure and be grateful for, many miracles; but they aren't able to be in contact with them. So there needs to be a family member, a friend, or a therapist, who can help remind them that what they're thinking of is no longer happening now, help them pull themselves out of the past so they can be in contact with the present moment. Why must we keep on locking ourselves away in the prison of the past? We need to return to the present moment, to be in contact with the miracles that are here in the present moment so that we can live. We shouldn't be tied down by the past.

When we use the practice of comparing, it's a different situation. We don't return to the past to be carried away by it. We just consciously take up the image of the past, to hold it up and compare it with the present so we can see we have so many conditions of happiness. That image of the past helps us recognize and appreciate the happiness we have right now.

So the capacity to create joy and happiness means first of all recognizing the conditions of happiness that we have in the present moment. Secondly, it means to compare the past difficulties that we've gone through with the conditions of happiness we have right now. Then happiness will come very quickly.

You may have a friend who is drowning in the past and who can't live in the present. Looking at her face you can see her suffering. You can say, "A penny for your thoughts." We help to pull that person out of the past. "Oh, today it's such a beautiful day; it's like spring has come." It can help take that person out of the past so she can be in contact with the miracles of life in the present moment. We can create joy and happiness for ourselves as well as for another person. That's not something very difficult. We just need some practice. If we're able to do it once, we can do it many times throughout the day. With each step, each breath, each smile, we can create happiness and joy.

Past and Future Are Available in the Present

You can touch the past through the present, because the present contains the past. You can even change the past. The wounds and suffering of the past linger on in you today, and you may touch them and transform them. We can transform the future also. With the insight of nondiscrimination, you can see that the future is here in the present. You can see that your children and grandchildren are already there inside you, even if they haven't been born yet.

When you look at a lemon tree in winter, it doesn't yet have leaves, blossoms, or lemons. But looking deeply, you can see the presence of the leaves, blossoms, and lemons in the lemon tree. When you look at a young man or woman who has no children yet, you know their children are already there in him and in her. You're in touch with the future. The future and the past are fully there in the present. With the energy of mindfulness, concentration, and insight you have access to the past and the future. We can train ourselves to see things in this way. It may seem strange at first. But we have to train ourselves to see things in the light of interconnectedness and interbeing, in the light of emptiness, nonself, and nondiscrimination.

A Story about the Dharma Body

Dharma is a word for Buddhist teachings. The practice energy you generate is also called your Dharma body, *dharmakaya*. One day the Buddha visited his disciple Vaikali as he was dying. The Buddha wanted to help him die peacefully. He asked, "Vaikali, do you regret anything?" Vaikali said, "No, I don't regret anything. I am very satisfied with the life of a monk. I only regret that I'm so sick I can't go to Vulture Peak to sit in front of you and look at you as I listen to your Dharma talk." Vaikali was very attached to the Buddha. One time he even had tried to commit suicide because the Buddha wouldn't allow him to be his attendant. The Buddha had seen that there was a little bit too much attachment. But finally the Buddha was able to help him let go, and he practiced well as a monk.

The Buddha said, "Vaikali, this physical body of mine is not important. It will disintegrate one day. It is my Dharma body that is important. My Dharma body will continue for a long time. My Dharma body is already in you and in many other people."

Every one of us has a physical body that will disintegrate. But we also have our Dharma body, the body of our practice. If our Dharma body is solid, is good, we don't have to be afraid of anything, because with our Dharma body we can resolve many difficulties. Every one of us should nourish our Dharma body, so that it becomes solid and strong.

Living Dharma

When we develop our Dharma bodies, we can deal with the difficulties that arise in our lives. Everyone should have a spiritual dimension in his or her life. If our Dharma body isn't yet solid enough, we have to try to help it grow. We do this by applying into our daily life the things that we have learned. When we walk, we walk in such a way that we can produce joy, happiness, and peace. When we observe, we look in such a way that compassion is there in our look. Compassion and understanding should be there whenever we work with someone, whenever we speak or listen to someone. By practicing like this, our Dharma body grows. We can help each other by nourishing the Dharma body in each other.

The Dharma should be the living Dharma. When you breathe in, if your in-breath has mindfulness, concentration, and insight, if your in-breath can produce joy, then that is the living Dharma. You don't say anything, and yet that is the Dharma. You're giving a Dharma talk without any words, because you're breathing in properly and generating peace, joy, and concentration.

The living Dharma is different from the spoken Dharma and the written Dharma. The written Dharma and the spoken Dharma are really only there to help us generate the living Dharma. We should live our daily life in such a way that the living Dharma always inhabits us every moment. Brushing our teeth, taking a shower, cooking our breakfast—we do these things in such a way that the living Dharma is with us all the time. We have mindfulness, concentration, insight, joy, peace, happiness, and the capacity to handle pain. We need the living Dharma. When we practice mindfulness, we can find many ways to make the living Dharma present with us in our daily life.

The Physical Body

I know that my physical body is not going to last very long. But I also know that my Dharma body is strong enough to continue. Sitting here I can see my Dharma body in China, Vietnam,

Indonesia, and many other places. Anytime someone takes the teachings of Plum Village and shares them with others, I am there. Everywhere, my friends are practicing walking mindfully, breathing mindfully, smiling, and generating joy and peace. So my Dharma body is going to last a very long time. Consider the Dharma body of the Buddha. The Buddha is still here, available. If you want to get in touch with the Buddha, it's easy. Just by breathing in and out mindfully a few times, you can touch the Buddha in the here and the now.

Each of us is a cell of a larger communal body, and each of us is at the same time a cell of the Buddha body. It's wonderful to be a cell in the body of the Buddha. You don't have to go out looking for the Buddha anywhere else. You're already a cell in the Buddha body. Rejoice!

Practice: Touching the Earth

The practice of "Touching the Earth," also known as bowing deeply or prostrating, helps us return to the Earth and to our roots, and to recognize that we are not alone but connected to a whole stream of spiritual and blood ancestors. We touch the Earth to let go of the idea that we are separate and to remind us that we are the Earth and part of life.

When we touch the earth we become small, with the humility and simplicity of a young child. When we touch the

Earth we become great, like an ancient tree sending her roots deep into the earth, drinking from the source of all waters. When we touch the Earth, we breathe in all the strength and stability of the Earth, and breathe out our suffering—our feelings of anger, hatred, fear, inadequacy, and grief.

The Five Earth Touchings

To begin this practice, join your palms in front of your chest in the shape of a lotus bud. Then gently lower yourself to the ground so that your shins, forearms, and forehead are resting comfortably on the floor. While touching the Earth, turn your palms face up, showing your openness. Breathe in all the strength and stability of the Earth, and breathe out to release your clinging to any suffering. After one or two times of practicing Touching the Earth, you can already release a lot of your suffering and feeling of alienation and reconcile with your ancestors, parents, children, or friends.

Touching the Earth is a practice that is helpful to do with your Sangha. When you are with a Sangha, one person can be the bell master and invite the bell between prostrations. This same person can read The Five Earth Touchings aloud while everyone prostrates. If you practice Touching the Earth on your own, you can make a recording of yourself reading the text or do it from memory.

THE FIVE EARTH TOUCHINGS

1. In gratitude, I bow to all generations of ancestors in my blood family.

I see my mother and father, whose blood, flesh, and vitality are circulating in my own veins and nourishing every cell in me. Through them I see my four grandparents. I carry in me the life, blood, experience, wisdom, happiness, and sorrow of all generations. I open my heart, flesh, and bones to receive the energy of insight, love, and experience transmitted to me by my ancestors. I know that parents always love and support their children and grandchildren, although they are not always able to express it skillfully because of difficulties they encounter. As a continuation of my ancestors, I allow their energy to flow through me, and ask for their support, protection, and strength.

2. In gratitude, I bow to all generations of ancestors in my spiritual family.

I see in myself my teachers, the ones who show me the way of love and understanding, the way to breathe, smile, forgive, and live deeply in the present moment. I open my heart and my body to receive the energy of understanding, loving kindness, and protection from the Awakened Ones, their teachings, and the community of practice over many generations. I vow to practice to transform the suffering in myself and the world, and to transmit their energy to future generations of practitioners.

3. In gratitude, I bow to this land and all of the ancestors who made it available.

I see that I am whole, protected, and nourished by this land and all of the living beings that have been here and made life worthwhile and possible for me through all their efforts. I see myself touching my ancestors of Native American origin who have lived on this land for such a long time and know the ways to live in peace and harmony with nature, protecting the mountains, forests, animals, vegetation, and minerals of this land. I feel the energy of this land penetrating my body and soul, supporting and accepting me. I vow to contribute my part in transforming the violence, hatred, and delusion that still lie deep in the consciousness of this society so that future generations will have more safety, joy, and peace. I ask this land for its protection and support.

4. In gratitude and compassion, I bow down and transmit
my energy to those I love.

All the energy I have received I now want to transmit to my
father, my mother, everyone I love, and all who have suffered
and worried because of me and for my sake. I want all of them to
be healthy and joyful. I pray that all ancestors in my blood and
spiritual families will focus their energies toward each of them,
to protect and support them. I am one with those I love.

5. In understanding and compassion, I bow down to
reconcile myself with all those who have made me suffer.

I open my heart and send forth my energy of love and
understanding to everyone who has made me suffer, to those
who have destroyed much of my life and the lives of those I
love. I know now that these people have themselves undergone
a lot of suffering and that their hearts are overloaded with
pain, anger, and hatred. I pray that they can be transformed to
experience the joy of living, so that they will not continue to
make themselves and others suffer. I see their suffering and do
not want to hold any feelings of hatred or anger in myself toward
them. I do not want them to suffer. I channel my energy of love

and understanding to them and ask all my ancestors to help them.

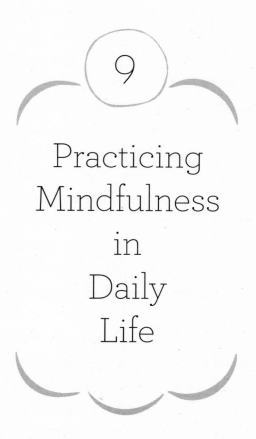

9

Practicing Mindfulness in Daily Life

Everyone walks, eats, goes to the bathroom, and sleeps. But your way of doing these things can be much deeper when you do them with your full body and mind together. When you walk, you are in touch with the Earth and the wonders of life. When you eat, you are more present with the food and the people sitting around you at the table. They will see the difference, and they will enjoy your presence. You can walk, sit, and eat in mindfulness, and bring your practice anywhere you go, but you practice by your way of behaving, without any outer form. You sit relaxed, beautifully; you walk joyfully, peacefully; you breathe mindfully; you look at others with mindfulness and compassion.

Mindful Eating

When we do sitting meditation or walking meditation or touching the Earth, our mindfulness helps us realize our connection with the Earth. Eating also puts us in touch with the Earth.

When you pick up a piece of bread, don't let your mind go anywhere else. Let your mind be there with the bread. To see that the Earth and Sun, the clouds, and the rain are present in the bread is very healing. When we sit and eat, if we chew our worries and our suffering, we can't heal. So to be healthy, we have to learn how to eat in a way that we're in touch with the present moment. It's not enough to be vegetarian and eat simple, healthy foods. We have to eat mindfully in order to heal. In short, getting in touch, being in touch, will heal us.

First we come back to be in touch with our breath and our body, and then with everything that is related to our breath and our body, including our mind. You put a piece of bread or some rice into your mouth, and then you need to have some mindfulness. "Here I am putting some bread in my mouth." Your mind should not be somewhere else. When you put bread in your mouth but you're thinking ahead to your job, that isn't eating mindfully. Seeing the piece of bread deeply, putting the piece of bread into your mouth, and paying attention to the bread, that is mindfulness. In a very short time you see deeper. You see the bread, the wheat, and the wonderful wheat field. A lot of work went into putting that bread into your hands.

With just a little bit of mindfulness, you see that the bread isn't coming out of nothing: bread comes from wheat fields, the sunshine, the hard work of harvesting and milling the grain, baking it into loaves, delivering it to the store, and so on. In just an instant, you look at the food and see where it comes from. You just look at the piece of bread, and you see that it comes from that beautiful field, the rain, a lot of work, manure, and so many other wonderful things—in fact, it comes from the whole universe. The whole cosmos contributed in order for this piece of bread to be there in your hand. That is insight.

You don't need to work hard to have insight; you just stop letting your mind be carried away by thinking and planning. Your thinking mind stops as you look more deeply into the piece of bread; that is mindfulness. When you look even deeper, that is concentration. Looking deeper, you see that the bread is a real miracle. The wheat field, the flour, the bakery—and finally the piece of bread comes to my plate. In just one or two seconds you have mindfulness, you have concentration, and you have insight right away. You have insight into the piece of bread you are putting in your mouth.

In your daily activities, you're so rushed to do this and that. You think; you plan; you are walled off from the present moment. It takes just a second to recognize that the wheat field, the sunshine, cloud, rain, the work of the farmer, the work of the baker are all there in your piece of bread. When you see that all these messengers of the universe have come to you, you are in touch with them. The piece of bread in itself can give you some physical nourishment. But if you are in touch with the whole universe through the bread, you are nourished not only by the nutrients in the bread but by sensing your intimate connection to the cosmos. You don't need any particular faith, any religious belief to receive the cosmos in every mouthful you take in: a piece of bread, carrot, string bean—so wonderful.

When you see where these foods come from, you feel full of gratitude. When you look at your piece of bread in this way, you're not thinking. You're not experiencing a thought but a view, a way of seeing. When you are present, you are in touch, and you see deeply. When you see deeply, you cut off your mind's tendency to be dispersed, to think of this and that, to be continually planning ahead for moments other than the one you're actually living in. You become more focused, and with this mindfulness and concentration, this ability to be in the moment, to be present with your breath and your food, you see that you are one with your food and with the universe.

Be present with your food and with the many things around you. When you eat, don't chew your worries, your anxiety, your planning. If you chew your plans and your worries, you can't be truly grateful for that wonderful presence of the piece of food in your mouth. When you are present with the meal in front of you, please also remember to be present with people sitting around the table with you. Don't close your eyes and only focus on your chewing. Open your eyes, look at people, and smile to them.

Mindfulness at Work

We need joy and happiness and peace to nourish us, and to help us transform the suffering in ourselves. When there is pain, anger, sorrow, or fear, we need to have enough of the energy of mindfulness, peace, and joy to handle the energy of pain in us. The two kinds of practice go together: how to generate peace, joy, and happiness; and how to handle a painful feeling.

When we talk with each other, we don't want to just sit and tell each other of our suffering and allow the suffering to overwhelm us. In a discussion about difficult things, the collective energy of mindfulness should be strong. When someone shares her suffering and asks the whole group to recognize and embrace her suffering, everyone should be able to use mindfulness and concentration to help her embrace her suffering. If we can do that, there will be transformation and healing, not only in that person but also in the rest of us who listen. Inside us there may be very much the same kind of pain. But we don't allow the energy of suffering to overwhelm us; we're not victims. We can generate the energy of mindfulness, concentration, insight, and peace in order to recognize and embrace the pain in the other person and in ourselves. So if you lead a meeting, you should know how to conduct the discussion in such a way that we all learn and transform, even when someone suffers and asks us for help. Practicing mindful speaking and listening, we can profit from the collective energy of the group.

There are times when we're working, we're lonely, or we're sick, and we lose our way. At such times we have to return to the Earth to be nourished. If you work inside a building, taking steps outdoors, if only for a few minutes, can help you touch the Earth and get in touch with more of yourself. When you open the door and go out into the fresh air, you're in touch with the air and the Earth. Each step outdoors is a step in freedom. You have entered the world of meditation. You don't have to be in a meditation center to be in the world of meditation. Every step is a step of mindfulness, of practice. When your coworkers see you walking like that, they'll be reminded to be aware of their own way of walking. Every step placed on Mother Earth can bring us a lot of happiness.

Even if we can't go outdoors, we can be in touch with the Earth whether we're at home or at our workplace. The floor may be made of wood or of bamboo. If we take each step mindfully, we're in touch with the wood, we are in touch with the bamboo, and we are in touch with ourselves. Whatever the floor is made of, it came from the Earth—so when we make steps on it, we're making steps on the Earth.

When living our daily lives, we need to live not only with our minds, but also with our bodies. Body and mind are not two separate entities. They're always together. We need to be present to both our body and our mind. As you go about your day, you may forget that you have a body. Are you truly alive during those hours? Or are you alienated from your body, your mind not with your body, during that time? We need to practice going back to our breathing and coming back to our body as much as we can during the day.

In Plum Village, we like to use a free downloadable program that sounds a bell of mindfulness on our computers. Every fifteen minutes when you hear the bell, listen and stop working. Breathe in, go back to your body, and remember that you have a body. When you come home to your body, you may recognize that it's tense. With just a few in- and out-breaths you can release the tension in your body. Then you can go back to work refreshed.

It's a good idea to put a bell on your computer to sound every fifteen minutes, so you can make it a habit to stop whenever you hear the bell and not just keep on working, working, working. Saying "Breathing in, I'm aware that I have a body" helps the body calm down. When I led a retreat for six hundred people at Google, I suggested this practice to them, because some of their staff work more than twelve hours a day on the computer.

Living Simply in the Present Moment

When we're working—whether we're putting tiles on the roof, preparing a meal, working in the garden, or whatever we're doing—we can be happy. We can be happy in our daily lives. Cooking, sweeping, and cleaning the toilet are all enjoyable things to do.

There are people who think, "How can I possibly enjoy cleaning the toilet?" But imagine how life would be if you didn't have a toilet. When I was a child in Vietnam, we didn't have a toilet. None of the houses had toilets. When I was a novice, we didn't have a toilet. Can you imagine that? A monastery with one hundred people living there, and not one toilet. We survived just fine. Around the temple there were hills covered in bushes, and we just went up on the hill. We were like the deer or rabbits, going outside instead of in a toilet. If you wanted to evacuate your bowels, you had to go up the hill. Don't expect that you'll have toilet paper when you go up there! There were no rolls of toilet paper up on the hill. You had to take dry banana leaves with you or use the leaves that were up there. When you had finished, you went to the stream to clean yourself.

We didn't have plumbing for tap water, we didn't have electricity, we didn't have a toilet. I lived in that situation and, in fact, I was very happy. Could you be happy in that situation?

At that time there were only twenty-five million people in Vietnam. Now there are ninety-nine million people in Vietnam. Now we have toilets; it's a great happiness. That's why cleaning the toilet is happiness; it's not something degrading. When we have mindfulness, having a toilet to clean is enough to make us happy.

Our practice is to enjoy that kind of happiness whatever we do. Cooking is happiness, because we have food, we have a kitchen, we have a stove right there. Sweeping is happiness. Washing dishes is happiness. We have the right and the capacity to be happy at every moment. If we can do that, we don't need to stress ourselves by trying to attain anything else. Happiness is in the present moment.

Once we had a retreat in New York at which there were a number of retreatants from Quebec. One of them later wrote to me and confessed that he initially tried to get out of the working meditation he'd been assigned. "When I first arrived, I was so irritated. I saw that the French-speaking retreatants had been assigned to clean the toilets." So he pretended not to know French, even though he came from Canada and knew French very well. He signed up with one of the English-speaking groups. But he couldn't escape his conscience, and finally he decided to join the toilet-cleaning group. While cleaning the toilets, he suddenly realized that it wasn't so bad; the comraderie in the group was enjoyable and it was actually fun to work together.

When you practice mindfulness in your daily life, you can always have happiness. You sit, you can be happy; you walk, you can be happy; you lie down, you can be happy; drinking, you can be happy; cleaning, you can be happy; cooking or washing the clothes is also a source of happiness. Practicing mindfulness is not hard labor. While working, you have joy and happiness. Whatever you do, the wonderful things and the supposedly unsavory tasks, when you're fully present and you look at things more deeply, you can enjoy everything.

We can have the joy and happiness of the practice in our daily life. The source of this happiness is our own mindfulness and concentration; it doesn't come from anywhere else. If we can produce mindfulness, concentration, and insight, we can have happiness. When we're fully present, our thoughts aren't wandering around in the past or in the future; we're not being carried away by problems, worries, sadness, or other matters in the present. When we walk, our mind is there with our walking body. Our mind is staying with our body because we have taken hold of our breathing and our steps. We are aware that we are breathing, that we are making steps. That is mindfulness.

The method of the Buddha is very scientific. It takes care of the mind and the body at the same time, and it understands that mind and body inter-are and contain each other. We have to do the basic practices for ourselves. Every step in walking meditation has to help us be in touch with our body and our mind. Every step brings well-being to body, mind, and spirit. Our body and our mind have to be there when we take a step. Only when we're in touch with our body and mind can we be in touch with Mother Earth. When we're in touch with Mother Earth, she is a very great source of healing. We can heal ourselves and heal Mother Earth at the same time.

Practice: Walking Meditation

Your steps and your breath are two very effective means to help you be in control of your body and mind, especially the strong negative emotions that can carry you away and take away your freedom. Your breath and your steps can help you come back to the present moment. There is peace in the present moment. You bring your mind back to your body, and when body and mind are united you're truly present for the moments of your life and you're the sovereign of your body and mind.

The practice is to be mindful of your breath and your steps so that you can be truly present in every moment of your life and have sovereignty over your kingdom—the kingdom of your five skandhas of body, feelings, perceptions, mental formations, and consciousness. Then when you want to speak or act, you'll express yourself mindfully, and you'll be able listen deeply and understand the difficulties and joys of another person.

When I practice mindful breathing and mindful walking it brings me a lot of happiness. Walking in a relaxed, peaceful way, healing can take place in body and mind. Let your in-breath and out-breath heal you. Let your steps heal and nourish you.

Wherever we walk we can practice walking meditation. Many times a day we have to walk from one room to another, from the car to the office, or from the bus stop to the house. Each time is an opportunity to use mindful walking to stop, relax, and be peaceful.

When I walk I sometimes like to use gathas, practice poems. One poem I use is "I Have Arrived. I Am Home." It's a wonderful verse to practice during walking meditation.

I have arrived. I am home
In the here, in the now.
I am solid. I am free.
In the ultimate, I dwell.

I adapt the verses by adding or taking away words in order to make the lines fit the rhythm of my step and my breath. Usually our in-breath is a little bit shorter than our out-breath. Breathing in, we might take two or three steps and say, "Arrived, arrived." It means we have arrived in the here and the now where life is available, and we don't want to run anymore. We have run all our lives. Now we decide to live our lives properly. Every step brings us home to the here and the now so we can touch life deeply. The natural world is here, the cosmos is here, we are here; everything concerning life is here in the present moment.

Breathing out, we might make three or four steps and say, "Home, home, home." This isn't a declaration; it's a realization. What's essential is that you feel at home. "I am home" means "I'm not running anywhere anymore; my home is in the here and the now." The past is no longer here, the future has not yet come; the present moment is the only moment we can live. Every breath and every step brings us home to the present moment.

As your breathing becomes slower and more relaxed, you may take more steps for each in-breath and out-breath. As you breathe in you can say, "I have arrived. I have arrived." And as you breathe out you might say, "I am home, home, home." You can adjust any practice poem to go with the rhythm of your steps. After practicing with Arrived/Home for a while, you can switch to Here/Now.

"I am solid. I am free," means that when you breathe in and make a step, you dwell solidly in the here and the now. You're not being pulled away by the past or the future. You're solid and you walk as a free person on our beautiful planet, enjoying the here and the now.

Mindful walking puts us in touch with the wonders of life. The body is a wonder of life, the trees, the sunshine, the planet Earth, and the sun, our star, are all wonders. When you're in touch deeply, you can go further and touch the ultimate. "In the ultimate, I dwell." Touching the historical dimension deeply, using the energy of mindfulness and concentration, you can touch the ultimate dimension. When you touch one thing with deep awareness, you touch everything. When you touch one moment deeply, you touch all moments. Touching the present moment deeply, you touch the past and the future. When you drink a cup of tea deeply, you touch the present moment and ou touch the whole of time. Through meditation, we see that the historical and ultimate dimensions are one. While living in the world of the historical dimension, we can touch the ultimate at the same time. Learning to stay in touch with the ultimate dimension, with nirvana, we feel a great relief.

You can use gathas when you do running meditation. Breathing in, you might make four steps, and breathing out five steps. You can always adjust whatever poem you choose. The main point is to dwell peacefully in the meaning of the poem in the present moment. Don't let your mind go far away, and don't try to be a poet and forget the practice. The practice is to cut the dispersion and dwell in the present moment.

When you walk, know that you're walking. Don't think about arriving anywhere. Know that you're putting your feet on the Earth. When an irritation arises, simply recognize it and say "Hello, my irritation, I know you are there." Say "hello" and "goodbye," and come back to your steps.

It's also wonderful to do walking meditation with children. They enjoy it very much and they come to know that mindful walking can be a calming refuge when they're upset or overcome by strong emotions. We can take the hand of a child as we walk; the child receives our steadiness and concentration, and we receive the child's innocence and joy in living. The child may want to run ahead from time to time and then come back to rejoin the walk.

Whenever I do walking meditation, I'm aware that I don't do it for myself alone. I know that every step I take will profit everyone—my ancestors, my students, my friends, and the world. Whatever you can do for yourself, you're also doing for other people. When you take good care of yourself and reduce the suffering in yourself, you are helping other people. When you're able to generate peace with every step, the whole world profits.

planting seeds of Compassion

**If this book was helpful to you, please consider joining
the Thich Nhat Hanh Continuation Fund today.**

Your monthly gift will help more people discover mindfulness,
and loving speech, which will reduce suffering in our world.

**To join today, make a one-time gift, or learn more, go to:
www.ThichNhatHanhFoundation.org.**

Or copy this form & send it to:
Thich Nhat Hanh Continuation and Legacy Foundation
2499 Melru Lane, Escondido, CA USA 92026

❏ Yes! I'll support Thich Nhat Hanh's work to increase mindfulness.
I'll donate a monthly gift of:

❏ $10   ❏ $30 ($1 a day)   ❏ $50*   ❏ $100   ❏ $_____Other

Your monthly gift of $50 or more earns you a free subscription to The Mind-
fulness Bell, *a journal of the art of mindful living (US/Canada only).*

❏ Please debit my bank account each month. I've enclosed a blank check
marked "VOID."

❏ Please charge my credit card each month.

Your Name(s)_____
Name on Card/Account_____
Credit Card No._____ Exp. Date _____
Address_____
City_____ State/Prov_____ Zip/Postal_____
Country_____ Email_____

www.ThichNhatHanhFoundation.org
info@ThichNhatHanhFoundation.org

THICH NHAT HANH is one of the best-known Buddhist teachers in the world today. His books, including Reconciliation, Understanding Our Mind, and Being Peace, have sold over two million copies in the US alone. He lives in Plum Village, in southwest France, where he gardens, writes and teaches on the art of mindful living.